Adopting Natasha

my first year as a mother

THE PUBLISHING COOPERATIVE

Denver

Adopting Natasha

my first year as a mother

By

Carol Lee

THE PUBLISHING COOPERATIVE
Denver

THE PUBLISHING COOPERATIVE
1836 Blake St.
Denver, CO 80202

Publishing Cooperative books are available at special discounts for reprint editions, bulk purchases, sales promotions, fund raising and educational purchases. Contact: Sales Department, The Publishing Cooperative, Finance Station, P.O. Box 480151, Denver, CO 80202.

Library of Congress Cataloging-in-Publication Data Pending

ISBN#: 0-9722741-0-3

Printed in the United States of America
Cover design by The Lightning Factory

The paper in this book meets the guidelines for permanence and durability of the Committee on Production Guidelines for Book Longevityof the Council on Library Resources.

∞

Acknowledgments

I could never have survived the past year without my parents and great friends. Now I know what Hillary Clinton was talking about when she said, "It takes a village to raise a child." Some of my friends, community members and family who helped me the most are: Karli, my housemate; Wayne, Vanessa and Erin, my great friends and neighbors; Alice, Dan, Shannon and Kate, my good friends; Harold and Claire, my parents; all the folks at the adoption agency; Natasha's teachers and therapist; and, of course, my husband Nicolai, his aunt and his daughter.

Preface

When I was researching adoption, I had a hard time finding any information on single women adopting older children from Russia. The stories I did find discussed the adoption process and the trip—but nothing about what happens when you get home. And that, for me, was the biggest challenge of all. I hope that my story about the adoption process and my first year with my daughter will provide some helpful information to single people (or anyone else) considering foreign adoption.

Adopting Natasha

my first year as a mother

I started investigating international adoption when I was 38 years old. I selected a U.S.-based international adoption agency through which a colleague at work had successfully adopted a little Russian girl. I decided on international adoption because of my age and my fear that the biological mother would return to take the child away. After a four-hour orientation and talking to several single women who had adopted international children, I decided to wait until I was around 45 to adopt. I wanted to wait and let nature take its course—that is, see if I would get married and conceive a child.

At 43, I decided to research international adoption again. As a result of a merger and layoffs at work, I found myself financially able to consider a new life earlier than I had anticipated. This time around, I went through the whole process and have adopted a four-and-a-half year old little girl.

I began with an orientation on January 7, 2000. I started a two-day adoption class seminar on March 7, 2000, and then I started gathering and filling out the numerous pages of paperwork. The documents I needed included birth certificates, marriage certificates, divorce decrees, medical forms, net worth statements, questionnaires, police clearances, psychological evaluations, employment verification letters, tax returns, copies of passports, guardianship letter, Deed of Trust for my house, six letters of recommendation, and my autobiography.

As a single woman, my international country choices were essentially Russia, the Philippines, China, Romania, Guatemala, Mexico, Haiti, Ukraine and Moldova. It seemed very natural to me to select an Eastern European country. I was very interested in Russia, Romania, Ukraine and Moldova. I think I was interested in Eastern Europe because I was exposed early to European culture and languages, as I lived my first 10 years in Copenhagen, Denmark, where I was born, and subsequently, Norrkoping, Sweden, and Brussels, Belgium. In addition my father is from Norrkoping, Sweden, so I was raised with a lot of Swedish customs and values. Also, during the orientation sessions, I realized that it would be easier for me to adopt a child who looked more like me and who was closer to my ethnic background.

After many discussions with the adoption agency, I ended up choosing Russia. At the time, Russia was the smoothest process to get through, had basically healthy children and accepted single women.

During that summer, however, power changed hands in the government, and all Russian adoptions came to a screeching halt. The government did not want to let any more Russian children leave the country, and wanted to halt what was perceived as the system's corruption. All adoption agencies had to become accredited for Russian adoptions. Needless to say, things slowed down considerably on the Russian adoption front.

In the fall of 2000, I heard that independent adoptions had resumed from Russia during the national accreditation process. So, non-accredited agencies were enabling adoptions. In these cases, the child is matched with the parent(s) by the Russian Ministry of Education rather than by the adoption agency. Instead of getting pictures and video, deciding on the child, and then going to pick up the child within one visit, a two-trip process was put into place. The adoptive parent/parents would sometimes receive a picture in the States, then the parents would visit the child in the orphanage. If the parents decided to go ahead with it, they could pick up the child on a second trip. Instead of waiting even longer, I chose the two-trip process.

To respect and protect individual privacy, American professionals and most Russian names and photographs are not included in this story.

My Background

My largest concern about adopting was always the idea of adopting by myself. I had dreamt of having a child with a husband. I still struggled with this while I was pursuing this Russian adoption. I knew I wouldn't know what would be right for me until I went to Russia and met the child, or children. Then, I figured, I would know if I really can do this by myself or not.

On September 8, 2000, I was laid off from the large telecommunications company that had been my employer for 14 years. I had also just ended a short-term relationship. Instead of feeling remorse over these apparent losses, however, I felt liberated. I realized that despite years of career building and an assortment of romantic relationships, I had never really found my calling in life. And I needed to do it.

How did I get to this juncture in my life? Like many career-minded women before me, I did what I was supposed to do. I worked hard at pleasing parents, friends, society, my employer and mainstream America, without question. In time, though, I started feeling emptiness, anxiety and a yearning for inner peace. My whole life, all I had really wanted was to be married and have a family. I could not figure out why that was so hard to achieve.

Of course, at that point, money and stability were concerns. I needed to feel secure enough financially in order to confidently escape corporate America. I didn't want to fall right back in just to pay the bills. I had hired a financial advisor six years ago, knowing that eventually I would need a cushion to fall back on if I wanted to pursue my dreams. Over the years, I stayed disciplined and followed his advice for financial freedom. I saved enough cash to live on for one year.

When the inevitable merger-related layoffs came to my department, I stepped forward. Everything seemed right. I had money in the bank and the opportunity to "quit without quitting." It was time to move on.

I went to Belize for a private retreat on December 10, 2000, and returned on December 19. When I came home, I had urgent messages waiting for me. Russia had sent my local adoption agency a notice that I had been matched with two Russian children: Natalia and Alexander. Both children were four-and-a-half and located in the Bryansk region. Bryansk is a six-hour train ride west of Moscow. I requested more information on both children. There was more information on Natalia and hardly any information on Alexander.

Beginning on December 19, 2000, I started praying and asking for a sign to tell me what I should do. The next week, I visited various daycare providers to get an idea of costs. The education director at one place, St. Johns Lutheran Church, encouraged me to go to their upcoming Christmas services.

On December 24, I went to a morning service. I couldn't believe what I was hearing. The sermon was about missionaries going to Russia to meet with kids in an orphanage and teaching them the Christmas story about Jesus. One of the little boys in the orphanage assembled the manger and had everything right, except for two babies in the crib. When the missionary asked why there were two babies in the crib, he said, "I didn't have a gift to bring Jesus, so I asked if I could give him my body to warm Jesus. And Jesus said, 'Yes.' That is why there are two babies in the manger." There was my sign. I said to myself, "Okay, I'm going." As I was leaving the church, I saw the director of education, and she said, "I think that sermon was for you." I agreed. On Christmas day, I told this story to my parents and declared that I had to go and see for myself. They agreed and were very supportive of my decision.

I decided to go see the Russian children I had been matched with. I set up an appointment with the International Adoption Clinic at Children's Hospital. I met with a panel of experts on

Russian adoption (physician, physical therapist, therapist, etc.) to look over Natalia's medical records and description on her disposition.

After three weeks, I decided that two children was one too many to begin with and changed my request to visit only Natalia. During the last week of January, I received the invitation letter from Russian to travel there from January 28 to February 28, 2001. I immediately sent my Russian visa application to the Russian Embassy. I asked to go to Russia for the week of February 19-26.

On February 2, 2001, my trip was confirmed, and I felt every possible feeling I could feel. I felt scared, excited, overwhelmed, and anxious. I think I called every person I knew, just to talk to someone and get these feelings off my chest. Then the next week, I relaxed and became excited about going to meet Natalia. I bought all my gifts for the host families, drivers and interpreters. I also had fun buying toys and games for Natalia and the other kids at the orphanage.

Then one morning I read some horror stories about Russian adopted children in the *Denver Post*. I was up all that night with nightmares.

February 8, 2001

It's 11 days before my trip, and I'm feeling neutral, and very cautious. I know myself. I must go down the path until the end, and then the answer will be very clear. I feel there is only a 50 percent chance that I will adopt one of these children. I need to feel a connection, and I have to know it's the right thing to do...for me.

Adopting a Russian child has been the most controversial subject I have ever experienced, especially as a single parent. I can't believe how many people say things like, "It will change your life; it's a large responsibility; maybe you should wait a while longer." Then they describe all the problems I might face. In addition, people want to point out the negative, and they all ask if I have thought this over. Friends and family members, people I have admired all my life, my mentors—everyone important to me feels the need to point out the negative. This has really hurt my feelings. Everyone tells me that they love me, and they are just trying to protect me. I'm 44 years old; I think I'm a big girl now.

What I don't understand is why more people aren't supportive of my journey to pursue this opportunity. If I were married or pregnant, everyone would be so happy for my new life. Friends and family would be throwing me baby showers and asking how they can help. As a single person, I am not receiving any of this. People would certainly not be saying the things they are saying to me now. I'm scared enough, and I have researched everything to death. What I need now is support and loving kindness. I don't understand why people won't look at the positive with me. I believe that I can make a difference in the world by bringing a child out of an orphanage and into my home. I truly believe the child will have a better life, and I also will be more fulfilled. Yes, it's unconventional, but so what?

A friend of mine had an interesting observation. He said that it's mostly my single friends or family members who have never had their own children who are questioning my decision. Most of my friends and family members who have children are very supportive. My friends who are most open-minded, compassionate and encouraging have small children. I thank all my supportive friends for being with me in my journey.

February 16, 2001

I have received some awesome e-mails and phone calls from people supporting me. Here is an example of a fabulous e-mail with the subject line, "Hidden Treasures. . ." from my Uncle Anders in Chicago.

Hi Carol,

I am impressed by your determination and actions in your alternative thoughts process. What hidden treasures may be found by expanding one's views? You are a living example. My thoughts go with you on your Russian venture and where you, no doubt, will benefit from new contacts and developments beyond that of gaining a lovely daughter. Please, count me in as an enthusiastic collaborator in your endeavors.

Dear Carol Ann, Godspeed and the best of wishes on your way.

Love, your Uncle Andy

Preparing for the Trip to Russia

- Bought four books on Russia, including one on Russian customs, learning Russian in three months, and two Russian guidebooks.
- Took two Russian classes to learn basic Russian and learn the alphabet. I took my Russian classes from Olga, who teaches out of her home and is from Siberia.
- Read four books on international adoption and preschool-aged children to learn about four-year-old development and behavior, so I could know what to look for on my trip.
- Toured eight preschool and childcare facilities to see what was available in the neighborhood and how much it would cost.
- Went to the international adoption clinic birthday party to meet parents and their kids from Russia and learn about their experiences.
- Met with the director and his team at the international adoption clinic at the Children's Hospital. I spent one hour in a consultation to discuss Natasha's medical records and what developments to look for in a four-and-a-half year old. Also her height and weight were put on a chart to see how she compares to U.S. standards. Then the physical and emotional risks were discussed. The team suggested I buy games to play with Natasha to determine where she was developmentally.
- Contacted a couple from my adoption orientation, who had adopted a Russian child. We shared stories and information on Russian adoption. We also supported each other on an emotional level. I think Barb supported me more than I supported her. Barb and I also took Russian together.

- Applied for my visa from the Russian Embassy in San Francisco. I enclosed a pre-paid Federal Express envelope to cut down on mail time.
- Checked the weather on weather.com. I nearly mistook Celsius for Fahrenheit. Still, it was about 28 degrees during the day and really cold at night. The streets are really slushy, so rubber boots are a must.
- Packed a carry-on bag with toothbrush and a change of clothes, just in case.
- Compiled a picture book of my house, Natasha's room, the dogs, the cabin in Grand Lake, Colorado scenery, pictures of myself, my parents, my relatives, the classroom at the preschool with kids, a map of the U.S. with Colorado and Denver highlighted. Everything was written in English and Russian. A good leave-behind piece should I decide to ask her to be my daughter.
- Set aside my video camera. Apparently, there is so much going on at the orphanage when you visit that it's important to see yourself with the child after your meeting. I also bought a disposable camera and a Polaroid, which I may end up donating to the orphanage.
- Filled almost two suitcases full with gifts—one for the orphanage, the other for the host family, the coordinator and the driver.

Gifts for the orphanage included:

- Dress, turtleneck, shirt, size 4T
- Jump rope
- Crayons and paper pad
- Sparkle glue to frame Polaroid pictures
- Beads to make necklaces
- Magnetic fishing puzzle
- A doll and clothes
- Four stuffed animals (As it turned out, the orphanage had a lot of stuffed animals.)
- Six-pack of blow bubbles (A huge hit.)
- Inflatable beach ball

- Two bags of suckers (Also a huge hit.)

Gifts for the driver, host family and coordinator included:

- Driver—carton of Marlboro cigarettes (highly appreciated). Apparently, U.S. cigarettes are different than Russian ones, even though the cartons look the same.
- Host family and Coordinator—brownie mix, CD player with lots of batteries, CD's, scented candles, potato peeler, grater for potatoes and sauerkraut with a container, picture frame, Cross pen and pencil (for the director of education).

Also:

- Checked to be sure I had enough frequent flyer points for trip to Moscow.
- Showed friends and family an adoption tape of another family going to Russia so they could be more involved and have an idea what the trip would be like.
- Established a communication team: one coordinator to communicate with by email or phone. This way, I could easily let everyone know that I was safe and what was happening. Also, the director at the international adoption clinic let me know he would be available for questions, if I had any once I was over there.

I would like to plan my itinerary before I leave, but it is impossible. All I know is that a driver will meet me at the airport when I get out of customs. Then, from what everyone tells me, you go with the flow from there.

I am having a hard time deciding whether I should bring a more formal long black coat or a down ski jacket. (I ended up choosing the ski jacket and regretting it because Russians dress more formally than we do in the States. My adoption coordinator wore a dark dress every day with a long coat. Had I as well, I would have fit in better.)

Tips for Russian Travel

There is a lot of mud and slush in the Russian streets, so it is customary to take your shoes off when entering a home. I strongly suggest taking rubber boots. I bought calf-top black rubber boots that I wore everywhere.

- Take tissue paper to use as toilet paper.
- Always carry your visa and passport.
- Make sure to have your visa stamped within three days of arriving; your hotel or coordinator can do this.
- Change some American dollars for rubles at the airport or at the hotel.
- It really helps to know some Russian and have a Russian dictionary.
- If you want to blend in, wear dark clothes.
- Use a money belt, especially in public transportation.
- Check bottled water for evidence of tampering, and don't drink the tap water.
- Make sure the customs people stamp your custom declaration upon entering the country. You might need to insist on this, if it's not stamped, you could have problems leaving the country.
- Make sure you declare your money when you arrive, so you can leave the country with your money, in case you decide not to adopt. An official in customs needs to see your money.
- Bring snacks for the trip, such as trail mix, chocolate, etc.
- Think of foods that are easy to pack and that you'll want to eat when you're hungry in transport.
- The host agency, as well as the drivers, coordinators, host families, etc, are all very wonderful people, and they are on your side. They also face a lot of bureaucracy and can't control things like appointment times. Patience and a sense of humor are invaluable.
- The most popular drink in Russia is Vodka. Through the centuries, Russians have been singled out for their heavy

drinking. Although a guest may successfully beg off drinking, the offering of a toast is nearly obligatory. (Vodka was never offered to me during my trips.)

Russians, as a rule, are very generous people. Russians like to give and receive gifts. The most popular gift is flowers, but Russians also give and like to receive books (especially fiction and illustrated art books), records, audio and video cassettes (both blank and recorded), chocolates, jewelry, clothing, electronic products, musical instruments, toys and watches. More often than in the West, presents tend toward the practical because of the difficult economic conditions in much of Russia. Foreign visitors who are invited to a Russian home will always delight a hostess by presenting her with flowers as well as with books, liquor, candy, cosmetics, fancy soaps, or toys, if there are children in the house. The gift should be offered immediately upon arrival. Presents in Russia tend not to be gift wrapped, partly due to the lack of necessary materials. Also, the gift frequently is not opened in the giver's presence. Some Russians feel that opening a gift immediately is a sign of inappropriate eagerness. Most people that you will meet at the orphanage make around $40 a month. So gifts are very much appreciated, as they aren't supposed to take money.

Tea is the most popular non-alcoholic drink in Russia. Tea makes a good gift. Earl Grey is a special favorite for Russians—loose leaves, not tea bags.

February 19, 2001

It's 8:15 a.m., and I'm on a plane to Washington D.C. I then take a plane to Vienna, then Moscow. I should arrive in Moscow on Tuesday, February 20, at 2:55 p.m. There is a 10-hour time difference between Denver and Moscow. Because of the many connections, it will take 24 hours to get to Russia.

February 20, 2001, Vienna

I have arrived in Vienna and have a two-hour layover. I didn't get any sleep on my flight because I was seated at the bulkhead, and the armrests didn't go up. In addition, I was seated next to a family with two babies that cried all night.

I definitely brought the wrong clothes. Everyone is dressed up in business clothes like the U.S. five years ago. I could kick myself for not bringing my long black coat. I think I am one of the few people wearing jeans and tennis shoes. I look so American. I'm surprised that the stewards are speaking to me in German. The international *USA Today* paper said that it is 25 degrees in Moscow today. I'm really starting to get tired. I'm sure jet lag will hit me shortly. From my past travels to Prague, I remember it's best to stay up until nighttime. It's much easier to adjust to jet lag.

February 20, 2001, Moscow

It's around 4 p.m., and I have finally arrived in Moscow. After I went through customs and got my luggage, everything has been a whirlwind. Nicolai, my driver, was waiting for me with a sign that said "CLEE." As soon as he got the car, we went to the travel agency. There I paid for two hotel nights—one for tonight and one for Sunday night. Afterward, I found out that I am actually taking the midnight train tonight to Bryansk. The hotel room was just to take a nap and freshen up. The adoption agency coordinator is going to meet me on the train. I spent some time with Nicolai, checking into the hotel, got my visa stamped, and then we had some coffee.

Nicolai is the nephew of the head of adoptions for the adoption agency in Russia. He has been a driver since he moved to Moscow two years ago. Prior to that, he was a businessman in Moldova. He has a 15-year-old daughter who still lives in Moldova, a 27-hour train ride away. Nicolai likes to fish, play billiards, read history after 1909, watch TV and spend time with his friends. He also likes to work, and he has been working very hard since he moved to Moscow. He hasn't taken a vacation in the two years he moved to Moscow. As he lives an hour drive from Moscow, his car is his first home, and his house is his second home.

After coffee, we went to check on my passport. It takes an hour after check-in to get it stamped. I also cashed some American dollars for rubles at the hotel. I then went to my room and took a much-needed nap. I had been sleeping for three hours when my coordinator called. I asked if she could e-mail my friend Suzanne to let her know that I had arrived safely in Russia. The coordinator said she would meet me at the train station at 11:30 p.m. After we spoke, I got up and took a shower, then took another nap.

I still have no idea what the plans are, but I'm sure I will find out from my coordinator on the train.

My coordinator speaks very good English because she used to teach English. Nicolai speaks relatively good English as well. However, I did get to practice more of my Russian with my driver than with my coordinator. If I rephrased a question a couple of times and spoke slowly, Nicolai could understand me.

I am now sitting in the lobby waiting for Nicolai to pick me up. I'm writing in my journal and drinking bottled water. All of the women are dressed up, and many women are wearing fur coats. They are mostly French, Italian and German, certainly not American. Everyone knows I'm American; it must be my clothes and my hair.

Nicolai arrives, and we are off to the train station. We wait in the car for a while until it's time to go. He shows me pictures of his daughter Natasha and his mother in Moldova. I show him the photo book I made for Natalia.

On the train I met my coordinator. As the train leaves at 11:30 p.m. for Bryansk, we have a sleeper car. It has four bunk beds. We get the beds ready with sheets and blankets. It's a very cold, windy night. As Nicolai and I were walking up to the train, it really reminded me of the Doctor Zhivago movie, especially the feel of the cold in the dark. My coordinator and I talked for about an hour before we went to sleep. There were also two men booked in our cabin. They remained outside the cabin until it was time to sleep. They slept in the top bunks. The Russian men are very respectful of Russian women.

My coordinator knows the director from the publishing company where she used to work. They have been friends now for years, and my coordinator has been with the adoption agency for four years. She really likes the people part of her job. She says the adoptive parents all have open hearts and are great people. My coordinator is married and has two sons, 16 and 19 years old.

I asked her what she considers the meaning of life. Her answer, "Love, to love all people. It's what is important in life." My coordinator was very interested in my coaching business. She said there is a great need for coaches in Russia because of all the changes going on. We also talked about Natalia. I found out that her formal name is Natalia, but her informal name is Natasha. Everyone at the orphanage calls her Natasha. On Christmas day, it was my coordinator who took the pictures of Natasha that I had seen. She gave the pictures to Barb and Paul Hansen when they were here to hand carry to Colorado, where the adoption agency saved them for me.

Natasha's mother lost her parental rights basically because she behaved as if she were single and childless. My coordinator said that drugs, alcohol and men are very common pastimes of Russian girls 19 to 23 years old. Natasha's mother just couldn't take care of her any more. Her father apparently wasn't around, so Natasha has known only her mother. My coordinator thinks we are a perfect match for one another. Natasha is one of the prettiest and healthiest girls in the orphanage. She is talkative and very friendly. The orphanage director told Natasha that I am coming to visit as a prospective mother.

February 21, 2001, Bryansk

We arrived in Bryansk at 5 a.m. and took a taxi to the hotel. I had some time to shower and change into a dress. At 8:30 a.m., my coordinator and I met with the director of education. This is the woman who matched Natasha with me. We received the permission slips for the orphanage. The education director still wanted me to meet both children, Natasha and Alexander. I agreed.

My coordinator explained the process before we left for the orphanage. If everything went well, my coordinator said we could start the paperwork for the adoption that afternoon. We are supposed to go to Moscow tonight on the midnight train. My coordinator said I could leave early to go back to Denver, or I could stay and go sightseeing. I decided to stay and sightsee. My coordinator also told me that when I come back for my second trip, I would have to stay for 10 days to get the adoption papers from Bryansk. After the court date is set, there is a 10-day waiting period should anyone protest the adoption. During the waiting period is when most families go sightseeing. My coordinator suggested that I might want to go to St. Petersburg on the second trip. After the 10-day waiting period, the child and I would go to Moscow, have a medical exam, then to the American Embassy for paperwork and visa, then the next day, head home.

At around 9:30 a.m., we went to the orphanage, and I met Natasha. We started playing games, made necklaces, etc. At the same time, I was supposed to interview her teacher, doctor and director of the orphanage. Natasha did really well. After about two hours, we had to go.

(I met Alexander—a.k.a., Sasha—as well while I was there, as he was in Natasha's group. The director of the orphanage knew that I was interested only in Natasha, so there were no hard feelings. And I knew that there was another family interested in adopting Sasha.)

Everything was happening so fast. I said I needed more time to make a decision. So we decided to spend the night, that way I could visit Natasha at the orphanage a few more times. At lunch, I explained to my coordinator how I make large decisions. First I need to collect as much information as possible, then I need to spend some time alone, sleep on it, then I can make a decision.

In the afternoon, we went to two notaries to notarize some documents for the court. The first notary was afraid to notarize the documents; the second one said she would (a gift opportunity). I felt bad because I didn't have any gifts with me.

At 6 p.m., we went back to the orphanage and I got to see Natasha interact with her classmates. She sang a song, drew a picture, recited a poem, and danced. We all danced the chicken dance together. I brought the gifts out of my suitcase, and Natasha handed out two bags of suckers. The suckers and blow bubbles were very popular. My coordinators photographed and videotaped the morning and afternoon experiences. After the pictures were taken, it was time for Natasha and the other children to go to bed. There were 13 beds in her room.

Before we left, we spent some time with the orphanage director, to debrief. I gave her my Polaroid camera and extra packets of film as a gift to her and the orphanage. It's hard for her to take pictures of the kids for adoption; she thought the Polaroid camera would help. The director made a copy of the Release of Parental Rights court document that was in Natasha's file for us and gave it to my coordinator. We left the orphanage at 7 p.m. and went back to the hotel. My coordinator went to meet her friend for dinner and pick up train tickets for tomorrow's train.

I had dinner in the café/bar alone and spent some time processing the day's events. I replayed the videotape in my room. That video camera was a blessing. Playing back the tape really helped me to see how Natasha and I interacted with each other. Also, I saw myself very happy and I could see myself in the role of mom. It's hard to feel anything when you are in the middle of all the commotion. I strongly recommend bringing a video camera with play back features. At dinner, I brought the Polaroid pictures that were taken at the orphanage and laid them all out on the table. I ordered a Pilsner beer, shrimp, some sort of very salty goulash and bread. I stayed for an hour-and-a-half, staring at the photos and generally absorbing the culture and the people. There were two live disc jockeys singing to background music. They were very good. I then went to my room and fell asleep.

It's now 4:30 a.m., and I'm writing in my journal. I feel really calm. Natasha has gotten into my heart. I was very proud of her showing me all her talent and affection. As we were leaving, Natasha asked my coordinator when she would be going to

America. She said she was ready to go tomorrow. For some reason, I always imagined having a blonde, blue-eyed daughter, probably because I was blonde and blue-eyed as a child.

I think Natasha and I were brought together for a reason. I think she will teach me how to be a mother. We seem to go together well, and I'm excited to go back today to see her. I think that is a good sign. Since I haven't been around many children, I don't really know what it feels like to bond with a child. Natasha is smart, cute, entertaining, giving, affectionate and well behaved. Natasha excelled compared to her classmates. Everyone had told me that she was the best in her class, but I got to see it for myself. In a couple of hours, we will be visiting the orphanage again. This morning, though, we will have only 15 minutes there. It is supposed to be closed due to an inspectors visit. I am going to ask her to be my daughter.

February 22, 2001

The morning went well. We only had a short time together. It was nice of the orphanage director to let me come visit Natasha again. Natasha was a little tired and confused when I was there. My coordinator asked Natasha the following questions for me in Russian, and added a couple of questions on her own:

- Are you happy to see your mom? Yes
- Do you want to be my daughter? Yes
- Do you want to live in America? Yes
- Did you think about your mother last night? Yes
- Are you going to love your mother? Yes

After she said yes to being my daughter, I showed her my picture book of her new home in Colorado. It helped that everything was written in English and in Russian. She wanted to take the book to her friends immediately and show them her new life. Natasha was ready to go with us that day. She looked confused and sad when we said she needed to wait for a couple of weeks for the paperwork to get processed.

I told her that I loved her. This word was foreign to her. They don't use the words "I love you" in the orphanage. So Natasha couldn't pronounce the words I love you back. She doesn't know what I love you means. I guess nobody has ever told her that before. My coordinator explains that we will be back. We took some more pictures before we left.

On the train, my coordinator translated the Court Decree Release of Parental Rights document for me:

> May 1999, Decree Release of Parental Rights
> Mother _____, born 1977
> Daughter _____, born _____, 1996

> Law Infringement Protection Department of IAD of _____ Region lodged a lawsuit against _____ concerning revocation of her parental rights in regard to her minor daughter, _____, d.o.b. _____, 1996. The reasons of the claim are as follows. The defendant abuses alcohol, drinks away the child's state allowances, steals, does not work anywhere and evades parental responsibilities for her child's upbringing. She was convicted by the _____ Region Court. Her child often stays in the

company of drunkards. The girl is often hungry. There is no food in the home. The flat is kept in disorder, it is dirty everywhere, there is no furniture. _____ did not acknowledge the claim. She explained that she would reform her behavior and undergo treatment for alcoholism. _____, a representative of the Foster Care and Guardianship Body of _____ Administration, supported the claim. She stated that _____ shall be deprived of parental rights because for a long time the defendant evaded her parental responsibilities for the child's upbringing and lived an immoral life. _____, a representative of the Commission responsible for minor children's cases of _____ Region also supported the claim and asked the court to deprive _____ of parental rights because the defendant did not reform her behavior.

Having heard the parties, the opinion of the representative of Foster Care and Guardianship Body, the conclusion of the representatives of the Commission responsible for minor children's cases of _____ Region, as well as the conclusion of the Prosecutor, who supported the claim, the Court finds it essential to deprive _____ of parental rights because it was established in court she evaded her parental responsibilities for the child's upbringing and negatively influenced the child. According to Art. 59 of RF Family Code, parents (or one of them) can be deprived of their parental rights if they evade responsibilities for upbringing of their children, abuse their parental rights or ill-treat their children, negatively influence their children by their antisocial and immoral behavior, suffer from chronic alcoholism or drug addiction.... At present she is convicted for stealing and sentenced conditionally. Her case is being considered in court. Therefore the court has legal grounds for _____ deprivation of parental rights. Following Art. 191, 197 of the Civil Code of Practice and art. 59 of the RF Family Code.

My coordinator discusses what it was like 10 years ago when Russia was communist-ruled. When the communists ruled, everyone had an education, medicine, a flat rate for rent, food was cheap and 90 percent of the people worked for the military. Now all the industrial plants are old, and the equipment needs to be upgraded. There is no money, no jobs, and not much military. A pension pays only $50 a month. There are refugees everywhere, and no registration process for them. The mafia and corruption have flourished. Russians are stubborn, she says. They want to live their own way and be self-sufficient. Russians are proud people and don't want investments from other countries.

February 23, 2001

Back in Moscow at Hotel Belgrade, I ate the breakfast included in my hotel charge. Nicolai took me shopping. I bought several souvenirs, four Matryoshka stacking dolls, a fur hat made of rabbit, and several watercolor paintings of architecture of the city. We went to New Cathedral and looked around and then went to the Red Square. It was closed due to military day. Then we had lunch at McDonald's. Since 1991, when Russia became a democratic society, McDonald's has grown from one store to 27 in Moscow.

After lunch, Nicolai dropped me off at the hotel and I took a nap. I went and replayed my video that I shot today, and realized that I had taped over yesterday's videotaping of asking Natasha to be my daughter. I feel so disappointed that I lost that footage; it was the best part of the tape. Oh well, I will just have to ask Natasha to be my daughter again.

February 23, 2001

After breakfast, Nicolai and I went to Red Square. I hired a tour guide for the inside of St. Basil's Cathedral. St. Basil's Cathedral is the crown jewel and heart of the Russian Orthodox Church. The Russian Orthodox Church split from the Catholic Church around 1550 because the Russian Orthodox Church did not want the pope to rule the Russian people. There were also some political conflicts. The Russian Orthodox Church is similar to the Catholic Church, except the doctrine is slightly different and the pope is not the head of the church. I loved St. Basil's Cathedral; it's very simple but elegant. The altar always faces East because Jesus was like the sun rising from the East.

It's fascinating to think that the communists could take away all religion in 1912 and gain total power of the country. After 10 years of democracy, today 50 percent of the people practice religion, compared to 90 percent in 1912.

Next, we went to the Kremlin and walked through five Russian Orthodox Cathedrals. These are mostly the burial grounds for the Czars. These churches are much more ornate. In the past, there was a Russian Orthodox Church every 1,000 feet. So most of the churches are very small and don't hold a lot of people. The communists tore down most of the Russian Orthodox Churches and used the remaining ones for storage. Almost all the churches have had to be refurbished.

The grounds of the Kremlin are very clean and well maintained. The price for a foreigner is three times higher than for a Russian. We also walked through the GUM shopping mall in the Red Square. The GUM was built in 1888 and has very expensive shops, with mostly high-end American brand names. The GUM also had some high-end German, Italian and French brand name shops. The government used to own all the real estate. Now the shopkeepers pay 20 percent of the rent to the government, and 80 percent has been privatized. You need rubles to use the rest room.

Nicolai and I had dinner again at the café in Hotel Belgrade. It had become our spot for dining. I asked Nicolai if he would show me how to drink vodka "Russian style." I couldn't leave Russia without the vodka experience. He said he would be happy to show me, but that he would have to park his car for the night because you can't drink and drive in Russia. He would have to take the metro home. Nicolai ordered half a carafe. The carafe arrived with chilled Russian vodka and two vodka shot glasses. He poured my glass then his, and we drank. I thought I would choke, but to my surprise it went down very smoothly. Then he poured another one, and another one. All of a sudden, Nicolai's English got much better, and we started having a lot more conversation. So the vodka kept coming, and we kept talking and talking and talking. And so the night went. When I woke up the next morning, I thought surely I would have a hangover. I was surprised to have only a minor one, not bad. Now I understand the vodka experience. The vodka is so smooth that you don't know how much you are drinking, and you can't feel it right away. But after a couple of hours it does hit, and it can hit you hard.

February 25, 2001

Today we are going to go to the Trekyakovskaya Gallery, where there are 50,000 paintings, the largest collection of Russian art in one place. But before we go, I am going to join Nicolai in picking up a gentleman from Michigan at the airport. He is here to meet his new 9-month-old son at the baby hospital in Bryansk. His wife is in Michigan with their first son. This will be their second Russian adoption. I asked him how the court process went.

He said the actual court time in Bryansk is an hour to an hour-and-a-half at the most. But there is a long waiting period until your time is called. The judge is usually a woman. There are two attorneys present, one for the court and one for the child. The judge usually asks the following questions:

- How do you plan to care for the child?
- Where do you work, and who will care for the child when you are at work?
- Do you have insurance coverage for the child?
- What is your support system for the child?
- How will you financially support the child?
- Why do you want to adopt this child?

It's a good idea to bring pictures of my visit to the orphanage to show that we met each other and played together.

We spent the afternoon at the Trekyakovskaya Gallery, then came back to my hotel, and I took a nap. My coordinator came by the hotel around 9 p.m. to finish some paperwork. A couple of minutes later, the director of the international adoption agency called and introduced herself over the phone. She suggested that I send notes and gifts to Natasha during the waiting period to keep Natasha interested and to show she was not being abandoned. She also suggested that I come back in three weeks to pick her up. My coordinator had said that six weeks was realistic.

After I hung up the phone with the director, I wrote three letters to Natasha, all building on each other. I also decided to give Natasha one of the stacking dolls that I had bought as a souvenir. Then at 11 p.m., a friend I had met on the plane, Corrine, called. She wanted to come over and visit. She ended up translating the letters to Natasha from English to Russian. I later gave the dolls and letters to Nicolai, who gave them to my coordinator. My coordinator gave the letters to the orphanage with instructions to give Natasha a letter once a week with a doll. I also stapled a picture of me (from copies of my visa) on the bottom of each letter, so she knew it was from me.

My Impressions of the Russian People

Strangers seem to be very cold and reserved. I feel like they could care less. However, once you get to know people, the Russians seem to be very passionate and romantic. The people are similar in some ways to the Russian architecture. The buildings are drab, cold, monochromatic and made of cement. But when you enter the building, the rooms are very warm, with plants, carpeting and enormous feeling.

The adoption agency folks are, of course, different. You are considered friends and family from the time you arrive. They are very courteous, kind, respectful, extremely giving and don't pressure. They just provide great service and knowledge. They are smart and hard working.

I was surprised to find out that there are 54 workers—all women—at Natasha's orphanage. With 58 preschool children, there are morning, afternoon and night shifts for teachers, cooks, doctors, janitors, and everyone else you need to run an orphanage. All the women at the orphanage had college degrees and were making $40 to $50 a month, except for the volunteers from the neighborhood. Russian women seem to be very attracted to volunteering to care for preschool-aged children.

When I took the midnight train in the cold and blowing snow, it was such a romantic and cozy experience, difficult to describe. I had experienced the same feeling when I was shopping and saw the watercolor paintings. That is why I bought some paintings; both gave me the feeling of being on the inside. I shared these feelings with my coordinator on the train back to Moscow. She agreed with me and appreciated my intuition and perceptiveness.

The heart of Moscow is very Westernized and very expensive. There appears to be a love-hate relationship with the U.S. They like our material goods but hate the fact that we have a stronger economy and currency as well as more jobs. The Russians are hard working, proud and very stubborn, based on what my coordinator says.

I have noticed that the Russian people are very emotional when they talk. They always sound like they are in a fight. When I asked Nicolai about this, he said they are angry and mad at everything. The Russians are not polite, not respectful, don't say, "I'm sorry" or "thank you." Everything changes if you are a good friend or family member. Then they are polite. Nicolai says that is simply how the culture is.

Moscow is the thirty-eighth most expensive city in the world. Ten years ago, it was the third most expensive city.

February 26, 2001

Packed, read and got ready for my long journey back to the States. I'm going to try to come back the first week in April.

I'm on the plane to Vienna reading the adoption agency notebook on the all the paperwork that I need to do before the second trip to Russia to adopt Natasha. It's a little overwhelming, but at least I'm coming to the end of the adoption process. That feels like a relief.

I was feeling anxious about all that lay ahead, so I made a list of things I need to do before I return to Russia:

- Meet with the international adoption agency in Colorado to go over court paperwork and find out what I need to bring to Russia the second time
- Obtain a Pediatrician for Natasha
- Fill out paperwork for insurance coverage and send in adoption paperwork
- Find an attorney to look over adoption paperwork for when I get back
- Get Natasha's room ready

- Register Natasha for preschool and kindergarten
- Show the preschool teacher Natasha's video and give her some helpful books, so she can teach her class a bit about Russia before Natasha arrives to ease her transition.
- Learn more Russian phrases
- Show the video to friends and family so they can support me in the adoption process

Now, I'm in waiting mode. I'm supposed to find out this week when my court date will be and when I should leave for Russia. I am finding it very hard to plan anything when I could be leaving any day.

April 4, 2001

I just found out that the court date is scheduled for April 10 at 10 a.m. I'm leaving on Sunday, April 8 at 9 a.m. I received notice of the court date on March 30. With such short notice, I wasn't able to use frequent flyer points, and flights were quite expensive. In addition, the visa cost $150 for a one-day turnaround. This wasn't in my budget, and the stock market has taken a huge dive, so finances are on my mind a lot. Today, I put my cabin up for sale to help with cash flow.

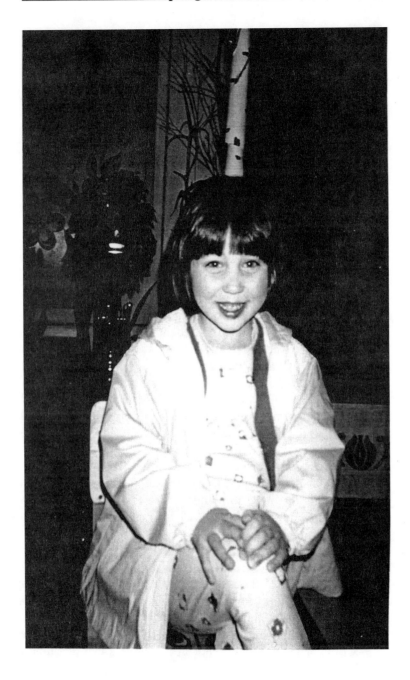

Second Trip to Russia

April 8, 2001

I'm on Delta airlines from Denver to Cincinnati to New York. I didn't get much sleep last night, probably only four hours. I kept tossing and turning. On Friday, all the paperwork finally arrived. The Russian visa and apostilled (another stamp of approval) medical form arrived via Federal Express. Saturday was spent repacking and buying Natasha some spring clothes at the last minute. I checked weather.com and the forecast showed Moscow to be 60 degrees. The turtlenecks and winter pants that I had packed would be much too hot. My Russian friend is scheduled to come to the house on April 27 to go over family and house rules in Russian with Natasha.

I will probably wait a couple of days when I get back to pick up the dogs and introduce Natasha to them. There is no question that the details that need to be taken care of for the second trip are three times more elaborate than for the first trip—and in a shorter time frame!

On the first trip, I had three weeks to prepare. This trip all preparations needed to be done in eight days, really five business days. And because of the shorter timeframe, everything is a lot more expensive. Plus, now there are two airline tickets, a one-day turnaround visa, the length of stay will be about 16 days now, as opposed to seven. As with the last trip, I have no idea what will happen until I get there. All I know is that this time I feel much more comfortable because I know I'm in good hands with my coordinator and Nicolai. I also have a much better feel for the process. Still, I am certain only about when I arrive and when I leave. If I go with the flow, everything will be fine.

I packed totally differently this time: a black skirt and jacket for court, another dress that I can dress up or down, two pairs of black pants, one pair of jeans, lots of tops, one blazer and one raincoat. I'm curious to find out if my wardrobe will fit in this time. I feel like I'm on a "business casual" business trip. I also packed several snacks for emergency hunger spots during transit.

As far as my feelings go, I have been very sad and angry. All my fears about having a child by myself have surfaced. I feel confident that I can be a good mother. My anger stems at my bad luck in not meeting a man to share a family with. I often ask, why not me? Everyone else seems to have a relationship, what's wrong with me? My anger is also directed toward my fate at what has happened so far. I am processing and dealing with the cards that I have been dealt, but I am angry that all the doors have been closed. I still keep my thoughts toward the right person showing up at the right time. I believe it's not my time yet. I'm just frustrated with waiting.

When asked if I'm excited about the adoption, I find it hard to answer. It's hard to get excited about the unknown, especially since I have no experience with children. I can say that I'm excited about coming to the end of this adoption journey and ending the terrible limbo. I'm excited to be able to plan, start a routine and get my new life going. I won't have to be waiting in anticipation anymore. I'm also excited to grow as a person in new areas of my life—areas that I can't even imagine. I feel that I am ready to pick up Natasha. I have no idea what to expect. I will just have to be very flexible and do the best I can.

I am now spending my flight time trying to memorize Russian children's phrases and checking over my court documents.

April 9, 2001

Arrived in Moscow, and I spent the afternoon with Nicolai and a woman who is a host family for American families who are adopting. Her daughter Olga lives in Denver and had asked me to bring some gifts to her mother. She served us coffee and cakes. She is a biology teacher. We also talked about Colorado and I think I have convinced Nicolai to come to Colorado to visit with his daughter. Later that afternoon, we went shopping for some lollipops and candy for the kids at the orphanage. At the grocery store, my handbag had to be checked in before I could enter. It's security against shoplifting. Nicolai and I had dinner and celebrated my arrival in Moscow.

I am sitting at the cafe in Hotel Belgrade tonight with Nicolai for dinner. When I came to Moscow today, I had no idea what to expect from him. He had sent me a couple of friendly fax letters periodically, but I had no idea what his feelings were for me. I was pleasantly surprised with his attentiveness and his openness to our future. Nicolai wanted me to tell him all about how I felt.

I was very happy to see him at the airport and to spend the day with him. I didn't know how I would feel, but my feelings at the moment are very strong. I told him that I would really like for him and his daughter to come and visit me in Colorado. And that I was open to what would happen in our relationship. Tonight at dinner, I feel really close to Nicolai. He had just made a toast about court the next day and me being a future mother. Even though Nicolai and I have a language barrier, I feel he is the only person who really understands me at this moment. I am really happy to be with him.

After dinner, I repacked my suitcases for my trip to Bryansk, leaving one suitcase with Nicolai. I certainly don't need to bring three weeks worth of clothes for a single day in Bryansk.

April 10, 2001

Today is the court day. We arrived in Bryansk by midnight train at 6 a.m. to check in. I met my coordinator in the Bryansk Hotel lobby at 8:15 a.m. We picked up some court papers and went to the orphanage at 9 a.m. A third-party doctor and a psychologist read over the new medical report and interpreted it for me. I also heard more about Natasha's family. She had lived with her grandparents for a while. Her grandfather was a carpenter, and he died when Natasha was very young. Natasha's grandmother continued to take care of her even after the grandfather died. Unfortunately, Natasha's grandmother died when Natasha was two. Several aunts then took care of Natasha, until they could no longer manage it. Then Natasha's mother took care of her for a short time. It sounds like Natasha's mother lived in a youth hostel, and the welfare inspector turned her in for being an unfit mother. There are inspectors that regularly check on children there to see if they are being taken care of properly.

I was able to spend 10 minutes with Natasha in the director's office before the court hearing, which she was not allowed to attend. She was wearing the pink dress I had brought her on my last trip. It should be very interesting communicating with her in Russian, since I only know about 30 words, and she knows over 2,000. She looks very happy and excited about me being her mother. We will be going back to see Natasha at 5 p.m., and I will be able to spend more time with her.

The courtroom is really small. There is a female judge, one attorney representing the Bryansk region, the assistant to the director of education and another woman filling in for the director of the orphanage because she is on vacation. There is also a court recorder. That is it. Usually only the family is allowed in the courtroom, as it is that small. My coordinator translated everything for me. The whole court proceeding took about one hour. The judge asked me several questions.

- What is your name, home address and birth date?
- Tell me about your family.
- Where do you work, and what is the address?
- What is your income?
- How do you plan to take care of the child?
- How far do your parents live from you?
- How do you plan to communicate with Natasha when you get back to America?
- Do you own your own home?
- Why do you want to adopt a Russian child instead of one from your own country?
- Did you meet the child, and on what day?

- Are you familiar with Natasha's medical record?

Then the director of the orphanage went over Natasha's family and medical situation. International adoption is the last resort for adoption in Russia; the government would prefer to keep their children in their country. The director of education explained to the court that there were only three welfare, or foster, families available to adopt in Bryansk. The judge advised me that Natasha would have dual citizenship until she is 18 years old. Also, a Russian social worker could request to come to the United States to visit Natasha.

Bryansk is a hard area to adopt from, especially for international adoptions. The city is still very communistic in its ways, and they want to keep their children in the country. After all the discussions took place, the county attorney gave opinion in my favor. Then the judge left the court for about 10 minutes to write up her final decision. I wasn't nervous at all. My coordinator was a lot more nervous than I was. All the pressure was on my coordinator, as she had to do all the work to that point. When the judge returned, we stood up, and she ruled in favor of the adoption. At that moment, I officially and legally became a mom. We did not ask for a waiver on the waiting period. I gave my gifts to my coordinator, who will give them to the right people at the right time. The judge will not take gifts in front of anyone because the court is not supposed to take gifts.

My coordinator dropped me off at the hotel, so she could go start filing the paperwork. After I arrived at the hotel, I decided to walk down to the river, where I am writing this journal entry in the town square next to the park. As I eat lunch, I remember what my coordinator has told me. She said the baby hospital houses babies up to three years old. At three, the children go to the preschool orphanage until they are seven. Then they enter boarding school.

I am now sitting at a playground north of my hotel. It must be 60 degrees out, and the sun is shining brightly. There seem to be many grandparents with small children. I think grandparents play a large role in Russian children's lives, much more than in the

United States. I went back to the hotel and took a nap. At 5 p.m., we went back to the orphanage to see Natasha.

My coordinator and I were able to take Natasha for a 40-minute outing. We found a playground nearby and stopped there. Natasha's favorite colors are red, green and yellow. She likes cereal, milk, pancakes, sausage, potato salad, apples, pears and fruit. She takes showers but has taken baths in the winter. She gets up at 7 a.m. and goes to bed at 9 p.m. My coordinator said she takes her vitamins. Natasha said she is really happy to have a mother. She is kissing me without anyone asking her to do so. She says in Russian how much she loves her mother and all the other children. My coordinator says she is in high spirits. She also told my coordinator that she now wants a father, a brother and a sister. I said that we need a little time for all that. "Please don't be disappointed if that doesn't happen." She is only four years old! She told me in English; "Mama, I love you." She had been practicing with her teacher all morning and afternoon. I can tell it's going to be difficult to communicate in the beginning, since I barely speak any Russian. I think I will be doing a lot of pointing for a while.

We then went back to the hotel. I had dinner alone. My coordinator met with her friend to finish the court paperwork and call officials for our return trip on April 22. The plan is that on Monday, April 23, we will be running around doing paperwork. We hope to go to the American Embassy in Moscow on April 25 and, hopefully, we will leave on April 26.

My coordinator and I took the midnight train back to Moscow. We had a man and a woman in our train compartment. The man was an international dance judge from Bryansk. He also is a cha cha and tango dancer. He is headed to Moscow to judge an international competition. He wanted to know where I was from. I drew a map of the United States and showed him where Colorado is located. On the train I gave my coordinator one of her gifts and a letter I had written her. The first gift was a pair of handmade earrings to represent her openness; the second was chimes symbolizing her love; and the third, a CD for her romantic spirit. I think she liked her gifts. It's so much easier to buy gifts for someone you have met before.

Nicolai picked us up at the train station at 7 a.m. We went to McDonald's for breakfast, but they only serve the lunch/dinner menu at breakfast, so I had a cheeseburger, fries, a diet coke, a cherry pie and coffee. Mc Donald's is a luxury for Americans because at least you know what the food will taste like. Then we had to decide what we were going to do for the next 10 days. After two hours of discussion, nothing was really decided except that I would stay in Moscow at Hotel Belgrade until Monday, April 17. One of the Moscow host families has a daughter in St. Petersburg. Tonight we will try to contact her daughter to see if I can stay there for a couple of days. All I know is that I really want to go spend a couple of days in St. Petersburg and see the Hermitage and the Kazan Cathedral.

April 12, 2001

From the *Russian Times*, "Although imported goods in other segments—food, textiles and electronics—of the market are of better quality then domestic ones, they are also more expensive and regular buyers may not be able to afford them. Price will remain an important factor determining buying decisions as long as the distribution of wealth in Russia remains as disproportionate as it is now, 10 percent of Russia's population controls 42 percent of the country's wealth. There is no middle class in Russia that can become the main consumer of goods. As long as the situation remains at this point, price will remain the main factor determining buying decisions. Since the 1998 financial meltdown, which made imported goods unaffordable for a broad section of the population, the ensuing gradual renaissance of the domestic economy has resulted in more and more Russians opting for domestic goods and domestically made foods, textiles and electronics.

President Putin recently reorganized the government. The Russians do not appear to be very optimistic about positive change occurring as a result. However, as one Russian poet put it, "One can only believe in Russia." The people want to believe and do hope for the best, but they remain uncertain that the government reorganization will lead to a fundamental improvement in ordinary citizen's lives. The poet continued, "Russians have believed in reshuffling since 1917. Former communists with new slogans have come to power, so nothing will be changed until a new generation of statesmen comes to power. Only people not infected by communist ideology can properly reorganize a government."

My impression of the Russians is that they are "night people." It seems that all the activity happens at night. Trains, planes, traffic and people are all busy in the middle of the night. I mentioned my impression to my coordinator, and she thought it was quite true. There must be some reason they have evolved to be night people. I wonder what it is. I will need to find out. It permeates the lifestyle here. The best time to reach someone by phone is 10 or 11 at night. I have noticed that people talk briefly on the phone here compared to the United States—only about one or two minutes. I think expense has a lot to do with that.

April 14, 2001

Here are some key points I have learned about Moscow. I feel braver about leaving the hotel alone and shopping by myself. My clothes are blending in more, so I don't stick out as much as an American. Also people are speaking Russian to me, which is a good sign. My Russian is getting a little better, and I'm feeling a little bit more confident communicating. I'm still overwhelmed by the language.

I finally learned to use the underground crosswalk tunnels to cross the street. I have figured out that the banks have various exchange rates for dollars. At this time, it varies from 28.87 rubles to 28.25 rubles per dollar. It's very interesting and fun to go to the grocery store and look at all the food available. It's so much better to buy some groceries than to eat at the restaurants or hotel all the time. The prices are very reasonable for Americans.

The Russian laws are changing for international adoption. The new process will require all adoptive families to take two trips, just as I have. In the past, Russia only required one trip. The visa process for Natasha at the American Embassy should go very fast. The American Embassy will ask a couple of questions on the background of the child and all documents will be reviewed.

So far here in the hotel I have met two new friends, Sergey and Jonathan. Sergey is the travel agent and coordinator for Hotel Belgrade. He speaks good English and Jonathan is his friend from Holland. Jonathan is here on a two-week humanitarian trip to Bryansk to fix up the orphanages with construction, blankets, clothes and food. Jonathan says nobody knows about how much radiation is left over in the Bryansk area from the Chernobyl incident. The whole region has been heavily polluted in the past, but there has been some major clean up of the waters in the rivers. In Moscow and on the train back from Bryansk, I noticed a lot of trash and garbage everywhere. The Russians are very educated people but not about environmentalism apparently. They don't seem to understand the effects of polluting the environment. Russia has high pollution rates, but they don't have the same exhaust standards that we do.

For the common person to live in Russia, it's about three times more expensive than in the U.S. But our expenses are about three times higher. The disparity is astounding. Most city-dwelling Russians live in apartments. The apartments are very clean inside, and their living space is much smaller than what most Americans are used to. I'm still curious about how people can live on $40 to $50 a month. Most people share their apartment with their family, so this helps with rent, but I don't know how they can afford to eat and dress.

I met Jason and Andrea from Phoenix today. They just adopted two one-year-old boys from Tula. They leave for Phoenix tomorrow. Their petition for the 10-day wait was waived, so their whole second trip lasted only six days. They said the visa at the American Embassy went very quickly. We went to a restaurant together and then on a walk. While we were walking, they told me they have encountered a lot of resistance from friends and family for adopting children from Russia. People are still sending them negative articles in the mail. I guess it happens to everyone.

My friend Corrine, whom I met on the plane during my first trip, called and we are going to get together sometime next week.

I made the decision to go to St. Petersburg alone even though no host families were available. I will take the midnight train on Tuesday, April 17, and come back on the midnight train on April 19.

Tonight when I got back to my hotel room, I feel flooded with extreme emotion. I can't stop crying. I feel so alone in the adoption process. When I heard that I couldn't stay with a host family because they had already accepted a couple, I lost it. Luckily, Nicolai is with me. He is holding me in his arms. I keep repeating, "I feel so all alone," and he replies, "Carol, I am with you."

Later, I asked Nicolai about the pollution here. He said that Russians don't think about the future. It's about what they will do and eat today. Pollution is not a priority in Russia. Russia was split up and privatized only 10 years ago. The economy is weak. When Russia was communist, there was a lot of talk about the environment, but if anybody did anything about it, they were reported to the KGB and taken away. There is no training in schools or the community. There are no government-funded advertisements. When asked about how long would it take Russia to do something about the environment, he said it would take 100 years before Russia would change that. It's the Russian way. I personally think it will take 15 years. All the kids in school are learning good English. There will be more international commerce, more trade, and a stronger economy. I think that as the economy gets stronger, people will think about their future and want to save money as well as the planet for their children. Right now they live moment-by-moment and day-to-day. Most restaurants don't even take reservations.

I also asked Nicolai how people could live on $50 a day. He explained that in Bryansk a person can live very comfortably on $200 a month because housing, food and services are relatively inexpensive. If someone says they make $40 to $50 a month, they are usually getting cash supplements as tips, donations, etc. to live on. There are usually two incomes coming in to pay for the family. There is currently no tracking system to pay for taxes. Employers do not take taxes out of each paycheck. Until a tracking system is in place, employers can't automatically deduct taxes from a paycheck. Russians do pay taxes on their wages, but it's impossible to track cash income. And Russia is mostly a cash society. Because it's only been 10 years since privatization, employee-tracking systems are just beginning to be implemented.

April 15, 2001
Paskha (Easter Sunday)

Today I went to Trinity—St. Sergius monastery complex in Zagorsk, 44 miles outside of Moscow. This has been a very moving experience watching all of the traditional Russian Orthodox Easter celebrations. Each cathedral hosted different services. In the first cathedral, I lit a candle and put it in the candle tray, kissed the coffin representing Jesus death and resurrection. In the second cathedral, I watched young monks singing A Capella. In the third cathedral, there was a full Easter service in session. The priest was blessing the congregation with incense. We spent about two hours at the monastery. I was really moved.

April 16, 2001

Today I was able to meet the director of Russian adoptions for the international adoption agency. Her story of how she began doing adoptions is a fascinating one. She has a Ph.D. in mathematics and used to be a physicist. She then worked as a technical editor for a technical scientific publishing company. This is where she met my adoption coordinator. At the time, she was a volunteer for an orphanage in Moscow. She was so moved by her experience as a volunteer that she decided to write an article about the children and the conditions in the orphanage. She received numerous letters in response to her article, and one of them was from an adoption agency in the United States. She ended up working for the adoption agency part-time while working at the publishing company. After 1992, the work grew into a full-time position. Since then, she changed adoption agencies to work with my adoption agency and now runs a very large organization with several coordinators reporting to her. She is hardworking, fascinating, smart and speaks excellent English.

We had lunch and got to know each other better. The director normally doesn't meet the adoptive families, so I felt honored to meet her. She has a presence and personality that commands respect. She's very direct and intense.

After lunch, we obtained notarized copies of my passport, the last of my court paperwork. Then I went to the Victoria travel agency to schedule and pay for my St. Petersburg hotel room. Afterward, we went to the train station to buy my train tickets.

I took the midnight train from Moscow to St. Petersburg. I was in a compartment of four. One American woman from New York, the director for the American/Russian Alliance for Women, spoke perfect Russian. She runs a volunteer organization to help Russian women business owners get started and successfully run their businesses. We also had two Russian men in our compartment. She and I decided to take the top bunks and give the men the bottom. One man was a translator for Arabic nations and spoke Arabic, Russian and French. He and I spoke French part of the time. It was quite an international cabin of English, French and Russian. The translator eventually became very obnoxious. It was apparent that he had been drinking lots of vodka. He went on and on about hating President Bush. Americans don't know what they are doing in the Middle East. They just bomb everything in sight. Also, he said that all Americans are stupid. My new American friend and I just agreed with him. The other Russian was a gentleman. Finally, the drunken translator stopped talking, and we could all get some sleep. I got to St. Petersburg about 8:30 a.m. A driver met me at the train station and took me to the hotel.

April 17, 2001

Today I met with the coordinator for the international adoption agency in St. Petersburg, and handed him the dossier that the director had asked me to bring to him from Moscow. We talked for a while. Also a former physicist, he met the director 30 years ago at a scientific conference. About nine years ago, he helped her with a couple of sightseeing trips for some adoptive families. They ended up visiting an orphanage and adopted two children, a boy and a girl, two and four years old. In those days there was no established process for international adoption, and the family had to do all the paperwork themselves. The coordinator helped them and ended up convincing the mayor of St. Petersburg to sign the approval papers. This is how he got involved with adoptions.

This afternoon I went to the Hermitage and walked around. I walked down Nevski Prospect Street to the Kazan Cathedral. I looked at some artwork, visited several cathedrals and found a nice café for lunch, returning to the Hermitage to meet my cab driver. It's much cheaper to get a cab driver from the hotel and negotiate a set price for drop off and pick up than to hire a new cab driver each time.

April 18, 2001

I am sitting at the Atrium Café having lunch and a glass of wine in between the Russian museum and the Hermitage tour. After the Hermitage, I will go to the St. Petersburg ballet at the Hermitage theatre. Then I will go back to the hotel, pick up my bags and head to the train station for the midnight train to Moscow.

St. Petersburg reminds me so much of Denmark, Sweden and Norway. It's so Scandinavian, and the Russian people look Scandinavian. The hotel, furniture, food, and ambiance are very similar and it reminds me of my childhood.

It's 5:30 p.m., and I'm at another coffee house waiting for the Hermitage theatre to open for the ballet. Coffee houses are a lot more popular in St. Petersburg than in Moscow, probably because it's a lot colder. St. Petersburg is a very artistic and cultural city. It's interesting to watch everyone go by and interact with each other. I'm looking forward to going back to Moscow. I'm glad I'm only staying in St. Petersburg a couple of days.

April 19, 2001

Nicolai meets me at the train station with long-stemmed red roses and kisses me hello. I ask if this is how he greets all his adoptive families. He said, "No, just you."

That night we had to drop off a couple from Scottsdale, Arizona, to catch their midnight train. I had spoken with this couple over the phone while in Denver and answered their questions about my first trip to Bryansk. It was nice to be able to meet them in person. At the train station, my coordinator, Nicolai and I talked privately for a moment. My coordinator translated for Nicolai. He said that he was making a decision about marriage with me before the end of the evening.

At 1 a.m., Nicolai proposed marriage to me. He asked if I was in agreement and said he wanted to be with me. He said he knew we hadn't known each other very long, but that he wanted to spend the rest of his life with me. I was in shock and decided to sleep on in it. At 3:45 a.m. Nicolai was scheduled to take another family to the airport and to return at 10 a.m. I went to the airport with him. I watched him with the family from Milwaukee and their new two-and-a-half year old. After the family left and passed through customs, I tapped Nicolai on the shoulder and said that I had an answer to his question. And the answer is "da," yes in Russian. He hugged me and said he was very happy. We both know that we have to face a lot of obstacles, language barriers, a move, and that we haven't known each other for very long. But we are both willing to go for it.

Later that day, we picked up my fiancé's daughter Natasha and mother from the train station. They had just traveled 27 hours on the train from Moldova. It's very apparent that Nicolai is very close to his daughter and that they care for each other very much. We then went to the American Embassy to find out more about visas to the United States. The next step was to get a visa for Nicolai and his daughter to come to the United States for a visit during the summer. A business visa was suggested, establishing Natasha as Nicolai's interpreter. We would follow up with a fiancé visa in the fall.

April 21, 2001

Nicolai and his daughter called at 8 a.m. for breakfast. We then went shopping at Izmaylovskiy Market, at huge discount bazaar, where merchants set up their merchandise—mostly clothes, shoes and purses—at about 50 percent less than in the stores. Nicolai bought a few shirts, his daughter bought a backpack, and I got a reddish-pink fashionable coat from Austria. This market reminds me of the Russian version of the Grand Bazaar in Istanbul. There were definitely no tourists here, and you definitely needed mud boots. After shopping, I met a man at the hotel that was the father-in-law of a man I had met in St. Petersburg. He gave me some instructions and the paperwork for filling out a fiancé visa. After reading the packet, it became apparent that we needed some romantic pictures of Nicolai and me in Russian venues. We were running out of time because I was leaving in two days to pick up my daughter. So we went to Red Square, and his daughter took several photographs of us.

We decided not to say anything about our plans to his daughter, but Nicolai did tell his mother and his aunt. That night Nicolai told me he loved me. I asked him how he knew those words in English. He said he had been studying. Now I have a new daughter and a fiancé who are studying how to say, "I love you" in English—absolutely amazing.

April 23, 2001

Later this afternoon we will go to Gorky Amusement Park. I told Nicolai that last night was my last night as a single woman with no children and the next time he would see me, I would be a mother. I have no idea how I will do or what I will do. Nicolai said that half the women are stressed and have no idea what to do as mothers. The other half look like they have been mothers for 10 years. He said you have no idea how it will work and how your natural instincts will kick in. He also said he would be there to help if I needed it.

We spent the afternoon at Gorky Amusement Park in Moscow with a family from Michigan. Nicolai and his daughter were also with us. There were Russian folk singers at Gorky Park singing Russian wedding songs. Nicolai said weddings in Russia last two to three days. Russia is a land of extremes—rich, poor, beautiful, dirty, clean, empty land, crowds of people, and so on.

Later that night I took the midnight train to Bryansk with my coordinator and the family from Michigan. They were adopting their second child from Bryansk. After we arrived in the morning, I slept until 11 a.m. at the Hotel Bryansk. Then I took a shower and was ready by noon. Now I'm beginning to get very nervous. I'm pacing the floors, so I decide to go outside for a long walk. I ran into the Michigan couple in the park. We return and wait quite a while for my coordinator to come back. The Michigan family said their court hearing went well and they had their 10-day waiting period waived. They thought it was probably because the little boy was the biological brother of the first boy they adopted. We will be leaving tonight on the midnight train back to Moscow. Finally, my coordinator showed up. We went to the passport office and signed some papers. Then my coordinator went around with her friend getting all of our documents in order. We met in the lobby around 4 p.m. By this time, I'm getting really anxious. I feel like I'm waiting outside of the delivery room for the baby to be born. I have no idea what I'm going to feel or what we are going to do when we are together. All I can do is go with the flow.

4:00 p.m.

We go to file the paperwork, get passport signatures, and pay for faster passport processing. The Michigan family leaves to get their child, and I'm scheduled to get Natasha at 7 p.m. after dinner. My coordinator is going to spend the night in Bryansk and finish the paperwork. Natasha and I will be able to go on the train tonight and share a compartment together. At 7 p.m., I pick up Natasha. I must bring clothes, shoes, underwear, everything; she comes with nothing.

April 24, 2001

We arrive at Moscow and check into Hotel Belgrade. We then go to the American Hospital for x-rays for T.B, a blood test and final doctor check-up. The whole process takes six hours.

April 25, 2001

We went to the American Embassy, but they would not take our paperwork because we didn't have a sealed envelope for Natasha's medical report. They wouldn't grant another interview until April 26, which means we will miss our flight home. We called to reschedule, and the earliest flight was May 2. After I called everyone in the American Embassy to help me, I was getting really upset and stressed out. By 2:30 in the afternoon, I had had enough of adoption processes. I said, "I'm done. Let's go to the circus and forget all of this stuff for a while." Later that evening, Nicolai, his friend, his daughter and I all went to the Moscow circus. The circus was fabulous, and quite fun for Natasha since she had been in the car waiting most of the day.

April 26, 2001

Nicolai, his daughter and I went back to the American Hospital to get a sealed envelope containing the medical report. We then went back to the American Embassy and submitted all the paperwork. We were then granted an interview at 2 p.m. We went to the interview and received our INS documents and visa for Natasha.

April 27, 2001

I desperately need help. I called the director of international adoptions in Russia to ask if I can have Nicolai help me. I am feeling so overwhelmed with everything, and not being able to communicate is really hard. She let me have Nicolai's time. We went to the zoo and had dinner at a host family's apartment.

April 28, 2001

Early in the morning, I got a phone call from my coordinator saying there might be a chance I could leave for the United States on standby. I said to Nicolai, "Let's go." We waited for three hours and, luckily, got on the plane at the last minute. I was so happy to be going home. We arrived in Denver and were greeted by my parents and great friends.

May 16, 2001 (Home at Last)

It's been three weeks since we have been back in United States and one full month since I have been with Natasha. Since I picked her up at the orphanage, I have had a lot of feelings, but I've had a hard time expressing them. It's 1:30 a.m., and Natasha can't sleep, so I'm up too.

I'm irritable, angry, experiencing a loss in appetite, and I have low energy. In addition, I feel like I'm running a hotel service.

We have both been sick for two weeks. I really need to go to the doctor and get rid of this head cold and find out what sickness Natasha has. Natasha doesn't have a temperature, and she is eating like a horse. Natasha is fascinated with lights and wants to turn on all the lights in the house. We have made significant progress in our routine in going to bed, going to preschool and eating at schedule times. It's still a little hard trying to figure out what she wants to eat. In response to everything, she says, "I don't want" in Russian.

I read an article today about post-adoption blues and depression. It hits 65 percent of all people who adopt. I think I have some symptoms, but not very severe. I've trying to balance my life and find, or hire, a support system. The preschool is extremely helpful for weekdays. I haven't been very successful finding babysitting at night. I have gone from having no children to 24 days in a row without a night off. I have found a Russian woman to interpret for a couple of hours once a week. This has been extremely helpful.

I have also changed my single status to engaged, so I'm not free to date. Overnight, I have taken myself off the singles market. This is extremely difficult since my fiancé is 8,000 miles away, with a 10-hour time difference and little communication. Now is the time that I need love, attention, and support the most. I feel very resentful about this time alone and having to fend for myself. I guess I must focus on the long-term gain for the short-term pain. I am also feeling very vulnerable. Telling people about my plans for filling out the fiancé visa documents makes me afraid, vulnerable, like I'm wasting time, and going to be hurt. I want reassurance, and it's hard to get it right now. I know I need to let these feelings go. Nicolai is not the answer to adjusting to my new life. I need to make my own adjustments, figure out what I need and make the arrangements to fulfill my needs.

In my new life with Natasha, I feel a slow and prolonged stress—totally different from work-related stress with deadlines. The stresses I feel now are my dad dying of cancer and having to start chemotherapy; having a child alone; losing my dream of being married and having a family; being responsible 24 hours a day; not having my freedom for a while; bonding and attachment; speaking Russian; being a good parent, setting boundaries and being loving; letting my four-year-old be a four-year-old

I know I will get through this. I will get over this cold, and we will be able to communicate. I also need to ask for more support from family, friends and professionals, and get more leads on resources to help me.

May 17, 2001

What is Natasha feeling for the past couple of days? Why does she like all the lights on in the house? Why is she scared to go to sleep at night? What does she want me to do?

I have been very angry at Natasha's behavior in the past three days. She doesn't like her food, clothes, school, and everything starts with "I don't want." I am having a hard time demonstrating love during her acting-out periods. Examples of her behavior are the following:

- She put half a roll of toilet paper in the toilet.
- I found poop on the bathroom rug. (She says the dogs did it, but it's all over her pants, legs and walls.)
- She opened up the back door and left it open all night.
- She won't stay in her room at night and is up every hour.
- She can't sleep in her bed.
- She has lights on all over the house for four days.
- She keeps hitting and blaming the dogs for her behaviors.

Things Natasha has done well:

- Drawings at school and mother's day gift
- Improvement in participating with the kids and teacher at school
- Playground playing
- Being with the dogs and playing with them

- Mom's routine, eating and overall adjusting to new situations
- Sleeping by herself for one week
- Eating some meals without a fuss

June 11, 2001

Creating a support system for myself has really helped my attitude. Karli, who rents my downstairs apartment, is taking Natasha every Wednesday night so that I can attend Russian classes. My parents are taking Natasha for three hours every other weekend. I found a Russian family to take Natasha for a weekend while I continue taking coaching workshops for my business. I also found a tutor for Natasha. I changed my priorities to putting family first. Natasha, then Nicolai, and then my business. I also sold my cabin in Grand Lake and hired an attorney to receive the stock options that I was entitled to. This has taken the pressure off of having to make money and let me focus on creating my new family. Once I made that decision, a lot of my anger went away.

I was upset at having the fiancé visa at the bottom of the pile and the coaching business open house at the top of the pile. Now they are reversed and in the right order for me. My communications with Nicolai occur every other day and are a lot more intimate. I feel much closer to him. A friend from my Russian classes introduced me to a book called *Wedded Strangers*. It's all about Russian-American marriages and the cultural differences. I found a copy of it on the Internet in Russian and sent it to Nicolai. We had some great conversations by fax about that book.

Update on Natasha:

- Attachment and bonding is forming.
- Sleep and nightmares still persist.
- She won't sleep alone. When she is alone, all the lights are on.
- We will see a Russian-American psychologist to help with abandonment issues and changes.

- She is starting to try to do more things in the house, and she is feeling more comfortable.
- She wants to pick out her clothes. I just need to approve them for the weather.
- She slept with my picture under her pillow when she was away.
- Everyone says she knows who her real mama is.
- She is practicing her English with the dogs.
- She loves her cartoon movies, my only negotiating tool.
- I have a better understanding of the food she likes to eat.

June 20, 2001

Today is Natasha's fifth birthday. I think it is the first time she has ever had a birthday party and gifts. We spent all day getting ready for her party. The theme was Barbie, and all her new relatives were invited. Natasha received gifts and cards from all over the world. My cousins in England sent Natasha a birthday card, letter and pictures. Nicolai's daughter sent her a birthday letter by fax from Moldova. At 4 p.m., the party began. We celebrated in Russian and in English. We had Cinderella ice cream cake with five candles with her new relatives and friends. Every one left around 7 p.m. Then a Russian woman from St. Petersburg came over. We were going to go out to a Russian restaurant to celebrate Natasha's birthday. She brought me red roses and Natasha some princess books. To my amazement, Natasha started acting out horribly. She started yelling in Russian that she didn't want me as a mother and that she hated me. The rest of the evening was a disaster. I felt really bad. Every time I try to do something nice and special for Natasha, that's when she hates me the most.

June 21, 2001

The day after Natasha's birthday, we flew to Boston to visit my friends Bob and Deborah. This trip was an addition to Natasha's birthday gift. To say the least, the trip did not go smoothly. Even though there were kids to play with, a pool in the back yard, and the ocean to play in, after four days it was extremely draining. Tough love and setting boundaries is emotionally exhausting. I was very lucky to have Deborah, my lifelong friend, to help me, but I was embarrassed and stressed to the hilt. This was the beginning of my realizing that traveling with Natasha can be very stressful. I thought it would be fun.

June 30, 2001

I don't know if I made the right decision to be a mother and adopt. I am worried about not bonding and attaching. I feel very frustrated and angry and out of control. I feel like I have lost my house, my bed, and my life. I have been sleeping with Natasha for three weeks and I don't want to sleep with her anymore. Her nightmares have gotten better. I don't know if I can be a good mother and provide unconditional love 24 hours a day. Maybe some of my friends and family members were right. I feel like I want to give up and not try any more. A lot of my energy is going out, and I don't feel like I have any energy coming back in. I am very scared because my heart is not opening up to her, as it probably should. I don't know what to do. I need to get help. I plan on hiring a Russian-American psychologist, talking to my adoption agency, and joining a support group.

I never thought about what would happen if we didn't bond or attach. The thought is overwhelming and very scary. The situation I have taken on is overwhelming. A five-year-old, abandoned and possibly abused by her father. It is difficult to know exactly what Natasha's past consisted of. I have mixed and conflicting information, which is typical in Russian adoptions. I was told that she has no father, but Natasha's birth certificate and some of the adoption papers show that there is a man with Natasha's mother's last name. We think that maybe he was a boyfriend or father. Whatever the truth about that, there was a male figure in Natasha's life who deeply frightened her.

We had a translation session with my Russian friend this afternoon. We discussed new sleeping arrangements and how to treat me in front of other people. She is starting to remember her mother and father and thinks that I'm her mommy "for now," which would explain her behavior toward me. She thinks Karli, my housemate, is also her mother. I told my Russian friend that we suspect abuse from her father, so she asked Natasha. Natasha said that her father would "beat her in the face" and her mother "would kill him." In the past when my friend had asked Natasha about her parents, she had said she didn't remember them. Natasha is starting to mix up her Russian with English, so it's hard to understand her. This is a good sign in that she is getting closer to learning English. Natasha thinks that her new mommy loves her because she had a birthday party, and she got lots of gifts.

July 14, 2001

Nicolai and his daughter did not pass their interview at the American Embassy in Moscow on July 3, so they are not coming to the States. Instead, they invited us to Moldova to join them on vacation in Bulgaria. We are leaving on July 17 for one month, returning on August 14.

Some important things I've learned about Natasha and me:

- I'm not a 24-hour-a-day stay-at-home mom; I suspected that this would be true;
- Preschools are a blessing, and they are the perfect break for me, and source of stimulation and other children for her;
- When Natasha is watching a movie, she wants me to play with her; Natasha wants to play baby during five-year-old games;
- Let Natasha play out her baby fantasies. It's a form of attachment with me;
- At five, her world is "it's all about me";
- Because of high suspicion of physical abuse from her father, I mustn't use any spankings or physical discipline. Even though she will test and try to get me to spank her, it won't work as well;
- She needs consequences, discipline, structure, and routine. This is very important;
- She is sleeping alone now, and nightmares have subsided.

July 18-August 14, 2001
(Trip to Moldova and Bulgaria)

Before we left Colorado to fly to Moldova, I made a videotape of a day in the life of Carol and Natasha in Denver, Colorado. If they couldn't come here, I would bring it to them. The videotape showed our house, the park, Natasha's school, the high school, Chatfield reservoir, an international adoption agency picnic, and hellos from parents and friends.

The flight from Denver to Frankfurt was wonderful. Then we took Air Moldova from Frankfurt to Chisinau, which was very interesting. As we are landing in Chisinau, I look out the window, wondering to myself, can I walk my talk? It's the person that's important, not materialism. We get off the plane, and I'm really nervous. Nicolai is at the airport with a dozen red roses, his daughter and his friend.

We make a couple of stops and then head for the apartment where we will stay. It feels really good to see Nicolai again. Nicolai gives Natasha a monkey toy in the car. We meet another friend at the apartment, and the festivities begin. For the two weeks we stayed in Chisinau, we were entertained and treated like royalty; we were either at Nicolai's friends' apartments or at a café. The temperature was very hot the entire time we were there, anywhere from 95 to 105 degrees.

The apartment we stayed at had no air conditioning or hot water. Also, though there were streetlights, they were not lit at night. Ever since Moldova was split from the former Soviet Union, electricity is scarce, expensive and imported from the Ukraine. The only nightlights are from cars headlights or inside apartment buildings. I noticed during this trip that light switches are very high up, so children can't reach them. I think this explains Natasha's fascination with light switches when she first moved to America. Lights switches were completely novel to her.

All of Nicolai's friends were very generous and gracious hosts and hostesses. It's not unusual to spend four or five hours, eating, drinking and talking. Nicolai was very busy translating conversations back and forth between his friends and myself. We spent one Saturday visiting two monasteries in the countryside and two prisons. Monks are still running one monastery, while the other one is now a historic site. The monks make their own wine. Nicolai and his friends talked the monks into letting us take some of their homemade brew with us. It tasted like grape juice wine.

All of Nicolai's friends were very interested in America. They even asked if we have lights at night in our streets. Moldova is a very poor country. I felt like I went back 50 years into the communist regime. It really makes me appreciate our government and our country. I think we take a lot of things for granted in our country. I learned a lot about "tradition." When I would ask why things were done a certain way, most of their answers would be, "It's tradition."

One day we went to the cemetery. The tradition is to drink cognac at the grave and reminisce with stories about loved ones. We went to the graves of Nicolai's brother, father, grandfather, and grandmother, putting flowers on each grave. It is bad luck to take pictures of live people standing by the gravestones.

Before we left Chisinau, Nicolai's mother had us over for a five-course meal. Her apartment is very clean. She is very curious to see how Nicolai and I communicate, as most of Nicolai's friends were. She was surprised to see how well we could communicate and how well I knew her son. We both agreed that Nicolai is honest, responsible, a good father, intelligent and has a big heart. We also agreed that he smokes too much and can be very stubborn. After our meeting, she told Nicolai that she is very happy for us and that she liked me very much and thought that we would be quite happy together. In fact, all of Nicolai's friends gave him the same feedback.

On a Sunday afternoon, we spent at a lake just outside of Chisinau. We swam and had a picnic with another family. A lot of Sundays are spent this way in the summer. Natasha had some kids to play with, but a lot of time was spent with adults, which she didn't like very much.

Boot Camp

Nicolai and I discussed Natasha's behavior and talked about discipline. Nicolai said it is very important to do something now, or as Natasha gets older, her behavior will be more difficult to correct. I said, "Please, show me the Russian way." He asked my permission to discipline her. I said, "Be strict. Show me—we have one month together, let's start now." So Natasha got a full dosage of Nicolai's boot camp. Of course, I copied everything he did. We had to be consistent and united, or it wouldn't work. Natasha gave Nicolai and I a hard time, especially at dinner and at cafés. She wouldn't obey either of us and said many bad words in Russian. The result was light spankings and time away from the group until she would say she was sorry. Sometimes it took 30 minutes for her to say she was sorry. We continued boot camp for the entire month-long trip. At the end of one month,

Natasha wanted to go back to America badly. She missed her house, the dogs, her new friends, grandma, grandpa and neighbors. She kept asking me when we would return to America.

Bulgaria

After two weeks in Moldova, Nicolai, his daughter, Natasha and I all got on bus and headed for Sozopol, Bulgaria. It took us 17 hours and four country border crossings to get there. Since Natasha was using her Russian passport, I was the only American on the bus. Natasha and I shared a room together, while Nicolai and his daughter shared a room together.

We were a family of four. However, Nicolai's daughter thought that he and I were there as friends. I found it very awkward that she did not know about our engagement. I had several talks with Nicolai, trying to understand his position. Finally, I understood. There were two reasons: 1. We needed to see how this trip went; and 2. In Russia they don't tell their children everything like we do in America. They wait much longer to inform them.

Our daily routine consisted of a knock on the door from Nicolai waking us up, then breakfast at the hotel, then down to the beach. There was also another couple from Moldova there that we spent some time with. We would have lunch at a café, play ping-pong, gin rummy, watch some T.V., and then back to the beach. We would come home, clean up and go out for dinner. We also did a little shopping in old town, went to the amusement park, and suddenly the 10 days were over. We got back on the bus for another 17-hour bus ride.

We spent two more days in Chisinau before returning to Denver.

On the flight home, I told Natasha that to live in America, she would have to do the following:

1. Go to school
2. Learn to speak English
3. Be a good girl for Mama

I asked her, "Do you understand?" Natasha answered, "Yes, yes, yes." (When we got home, there was significant improvement in her behavior and attitude. It lasted about two weeks, but some of it stuck. After three weeks, the light spankings were no longer needed. I said she must try to be good and say, "May I," "Please" and "I'm sorry" when she hurt people or animals. I haven't had to spank her very much. At boot camp, it was the only way to get her attention, now I don't need to do that to get her attention. Strictness works with her. I think she trusts the structure. Lovingness works for a while, but then she takes advantage of the person or situation.)

August 16, 2001

Two days after I returned to Denver, Nicolai and I decided to proceed with filing for a fiancé visa.

August 20, 2001

I am happy 10 percent of the time and unhappy 90 percent of the time. What makes me angry?

When I pick up Natasha from school, she doesn't want to go home with me, or she wants to go to someone else's house. She doesn't greet me, and she treats me like dirt. I am very embarrassed. She doesn't say hello, look happy to see me, or hug and kiss me hello.

After I have done something really special for her, like have a birthday party for her with lots of gifts, she tells me how much she hates me and doesn't want me as her mother.

She talks about wanting to be with the Russian family (who baby-sits her sometimes) three to four times a day. She says she wants to be with her mama, papa, sister and small cat, loves their house and doesn't want to be in our house or with me.

She acts spoiled and doesn't appreciate what she has.

After I ask her several times nicely not to draw with markers on her hand, she draws with the marker on her hand and face. She also likes to destroy toys and whatever else she has.

She sometimes doesn't obey and resists what I say—for instance, she opens the car door when I'm driving.

She sings the ABC's 102 times in one day.

When I'm stressed and tired, I lose my patience.

She wants to argue and control everything—hair, dress, movies, food, etc.

I'm always wrong, even when I repeat what she just said.

September 19, 2001

It's been almost five months since I picked up Natasha from Bryansk. Things are starting to get better. We are still on a roller coaster ride week by week, but I feel we are starting to bond, and our lives are starting to stabilize.

We began counseling a month ago. Natasha has a Russian counselor, and I have an American counselor who has a lot of experience with adoption and foster children. I also have found a Russian family to take care of Natasha once in a while for a weekend. Natasha started kindergarten at her elementary school August 20 and likes it. On September 16, she was baptized at a Lutheran Church. We told her it is a celebration for her to be with God. She now demonstrates the cross sign. Her grandparents and Karli came to the ceremony as witnesses. We then had a brunch, went to the park and had dinner at her grandparent's house.

October 3, 2001

Natasha's English is really starting to pick up. She likes school and enjoys getting smiley faces from her kindergarten teachers. The other night she watched the video that I took in Bryansk on my first visit to the orphanage. She started crying and named off all the children's names at the orphanage. She said she missed Bryansk and wanted to go back. Then she said in English,

"Bryansk is gone." I felt really bad for her, hugged her and said she could go back some day. Then I asked if she would like to write a letter to her friends in Bryansk. She did. So the next day we wrote a letter to the kids at the orphanage in Bryansk. I will fax it to Nicolai and ask him to give it to my Russian coordinator to deliver to the orphanage. I also asked the adoption agency if it is okay if I contact the family who adopted Sasha, so the kids could talk to each other on the phone. The agency agreed, and we called the family in Phoenix who adopted Sasha. I told Natasha's therapist, Lena, what I had done. Lena advised me not to do this and said that I was only hurting Natasha. I needed to focus on the present and leave the past alone. The past is best to be dealt with at a much later date. So, I learned my lesson, no more memories of Russia and her past for now.

We went to go get Natasha's Halloween costume last night, and she practiced knocking on the door saying, "Trick or Treat," waiting for the candy, then saying, "Thank You." She is going to be a black "Barbie Cat." We also rented the video "Rudolf the Red Nose Reindeer" to learn a little about Christmas. Natasha is now getting excited about Halloween and Christmas. It's giving her something to look forward to.

During the week, we seem to get along well; things go smoothly when she is in school. The weekend is more emotional. Ballet classes on Saturday have helped. There are still control and anger issues. I have decided some anger is good and necessary. I have also learned to really stretch my patience. When I'm tired and stressed, my patience is very low. I lose my temper, and I don't want to argue. I see that a lot of progress has been made. I still question if I'm cut out for this new responsibility, but not as often.

I researched attachment issues and disruption. There are times I wonder if I made the right decision and if I can truly enjoy being a mother. I met with the adoption agency and my therapist. Basically, as they see it, we are attaching to each other. We both are very anxious and stressed around each other, though, and our situation is called anxiety attachment. Natasha is in a new country, with new language, new people, new culture, new food, new caretakers, etc., which causes a lot of stress. I have gone from being single, free to do what ever I want, with lots of friends, dating, and having a career to a 24-hour responsibility, cooking at home every night, doing children's activities at night and being engaged to a man 8,000 miles away. This stresses me out. So when you put the two together, you get anxiety attachment, with a lot of yelling and friction.

When Natasha gets angry with me, she drains me. Depending on my mood, I can be patient, come up with a creative response or move on. But if I'm in a bad mood and I'm feeling stressed, I'm impatient. I don't want to put up with her treatment, and I tell her to stop it. This is the area that I'm trying to work on. The good news is that anxiety attachment doesn't last forever. It's one to two years, and then the attachment should be stabilized. Hopefully, she will stop wanting everyone else to be her family and accept the one she has. When Natasha stays with the Russian family for a weekend, she comes home and tells me about her papa, mama, sister and small cat. Or when she plays at her friend's house, she wants to live with mama, papa, and her two sisters.

I always feel bad because right now I can't give her a father, a brother or sister. I can give her only two dogs, friends, play dates and me. So far, I have put everything in place except for a couple of babysitters. I'm hoping to find another single mom and one child Natasha's age so we can trade off and have an evening off or a weekend.

In September, the Children's hospital told me I needed to cut her off from speaking Russian and really immerse her in English. So I stopped speaking Russian to her. It wasn't very difficult because she could understand in English almost everything I was saying in Russian.

My therapist also said to give our relationship at least one year. It is important to go through all the first's together—first birthday, first Halloween, first baptism, first Thanksgiving, first Christmas, first Easter, etc., similar to dating. One year together gives us a chance to bond and get to know each other. It is also important not to give up too soon because I could regret the decision later.

June 14, 2001 to October 3, 2001
(Administrative Work for Adopting Natasha)

- Hired an attorney to file in a Denver court for re-adoption in the state of Colorado
- Received court re-adoption petition August 7
- Went to Colorado Health Department and paid for Colorado birth certificate
- With re-adoption papers, birth certificate and Russian passport, I filed for her U.S. passport. It takes at least six weeks to process.
- Filed for social security card after I received the U.S passport as proof of U.S. citizenship
- Met with tax advisor for 2001 taxes
- Created 2002 expense budget
- Completed all comprehensive doctor, dentist and vision doctor appointments
- Found a counseling program for Russian immigrants that Natasha qualifies for
- Researched health care providers for 2002
- Attended Russian classes
- Signed Natasha up for one activity after school each quarter—ballet for winter, T-ball for spring, swimming for summer, and soccer for fall.
- Filed reports for Russia and the adoption agency (During the first year, every three months, a report must be written on Natasha's developmental progress, and 12 new pictures must be sent with each report. After the first year, a report and 15 pictures need be submitted annually. The report contains the parent name(s), date, current address, child's name, date of birth, placement city, date last checked by a physician, weight and height, any physical problems, section on child's development and how child is doing in school, favorite games and toys, and parental signature(s).

October 23, 2001

Nicolai and I have been faxing letters back and forth like crazy to decide where and how we will get married. After some help from his aunt translating for us, we finally decided to have the legal marriage and reception in the United States and the church wedding later in Moscow for his family at a Russian Orthodox church. Nicolai made it very clear that he wanted only one church wedding. After much soul searching, I decided that I really wanted the church wedding to be in Russia. Every time I am in a Russian Orthodox Church, I am spiritually moved. I get goose bumps on my arms and am in awe.

I also researched the Russian Orthodox ceremony and was pleased to discover that the church is rich with ritual and symbolism for marriage ceremonies. Each act has a special meaning and significance. There is the blessing of the rings, the lighting of the candle, the joining of right hands, the crowing, the common cup, the circle walk around the table, and the blessing. Nicolai was very pleased to hear that I really wanted the have the church wedding in Russia. I didn't know it at the time that I made my decision, but it is tradition that the church ceremony is in the town of the groom's family.

November 17, 2001

It's been almost seven months since I picked up Natasha from Bryansk and that she became my daughter. This is the first week that I feel myself really bonding and attaching to Natasha. I've noticed some signs this week. I had my first dream about Natasha. I think about her during the day, and I'm thinking about what she would like to do after school. I find myself going to the library to get library books and videos that she would like. I don't feel anxious when I'm picking her up from school and when we spend all weekend alone. I want to initiate hugs and kisses more. I feel an awareness of moving from caretaker to mother.

Here are some observations about Natasha:

- She is sleeping through the night, but always with the lights on.
- She is eating her food and turning off the T.V. without a fight.
- She is getting smiley faces at school for her behavior.
- She is better behaved in front of adults.
- Her English has significantly improved.
- She is not resisting and acting out as frequently as before.
- She loves going to school, and she is starting to have some friends.
- She is very good at doing things at the playground and wants to show me.

I feel more confident, and I'm not feeling as overwhelmed as I was. I'm not taking the rejection so personally. Natasha's imaginary family is even surfacing more often. She discusses her mother, father, brother, sister and cat all the time. She talks about the fact that she is waiting for them to come get her. I try to include her imaginary family at the dinner table. But sometimes I say that I am her new family.

My counselor says the imaginary family could be anything from her past or perhaps even kids in the orphanage playing different roles. Natasha's counselor said that she is neat and put together on the outside, but totally disorganized on the inside. She showed me a huge mess of toys and said, "This is Natasha on the inside, and we have a lot of work to do to put everything away in its proper place." I am forbidden to discuss the past until a later date, and I should tell her she is a good girl a lot.

Natasha knows I am leaving for two weeks to see Nicolai in Moscow in December.

November 26 to December 1, 2001 (Trip to Moscow Without Natasha)

It's Monday after Thanksgiving, and I'm at the airport waiting for my plane to Frankfurt and then to Moscow. The last four days with Natasha were emotionally exhausting. We stayed very busy, but she wanted my attention every two minutes, and she didn't care if it was positive or negative attention. I think she was trying to drive me nuts. I think it was separation anxiety over me leaving. Last night, she began crying as I tucked her in. I asked her to come into my arms and asked why she was crying. She said she was going to miss me. I assured her that I was coming back before Christmas and that I would miss her too. I also said that mommy has always come back to pick her up at school, after a weekend away, etc. I asked her to look me in the eyes, and I said, "Natasha, mommy is not leaving you, I promise I will be back." This seemed to calm her down. As I went to my bedroom that evening, I thought to myself. "I think she is attaching to me and that it's sinking in that I'm her mama."

It was great to have a two-week break from my responsibilities in Denver. It was also extremely important that Nicolai and I have this time alone together. I definitely lived on the Russian side on this trip. Nicolai and I stayed in his grandmother's one room apartment alone. We went to the market and cooked at home every night. I would either stay in the apartment or go with Nicolai driving for his work. We looked at a couple of churches recommended by various friends and family. We chose his friend's church for our wedding next summer. She and her husband had us over for a wonderful dinner, and the woman translated some final documents for the fiancé visa for us. Then two days before I left, Nicolai and his family had an official engagement party at his aunt's apartment. I also got to meet his grandmother and more relatives. Nicolai and I agreed to have our first wedding in Denver on April 19, 2002, and our second wedding in the Russian Orthodox Church, in Moscow, sometime in June.

During the first week I was gone, apparently Natasha didn't miss me very much, but by the second week she was asking for me, "When will mama be home?" Karli did a great job taking her to school and keeping her entertained while I was gone. When I returned home on December 10, Natasha was very happy to see me.

January 25, 2002

Natasha and I had plenty of time to get reacquainted. Christmas break started December 19. Natasha and I have spent 23 out of 32 days together during the last month (24 hours a day).

Natasha just received her mid-year report card, and her kindergarten teacher wrote, "Wow! Natasha is learning a lot. She has come quite a long way! I am proud of her. We are working on letters and sounds and the words that label things she knows like cat."

Her English is great, and everyone can understand her. People are amazed at her English. Last week I received an invitation to go to have lunch with Natasha and her lunch mates. I went and had lunch with the kids. All the kids said that she had told them that she didn't have a mama or papa, and then Natasha said, "No, this is my mama." It seemed like she wanted to show everyone that I am her mama. For me this was a huge sign that Natasha is accepting me as her mother. Natasha is starting to sit on my lap at functions in front of other people. She is also noticing how her friends are treating their mothers. For example, she told me, "Sela kisses her mother on the mouth, can we do that?" I said, "Of course." She is also starting to say, "I love you" periodically. Her nightmares have not completely gone away, but she keeps telling me new ways she plans to handle her monsters. She has tried singing to them, hugging them and beating them up so far.

February 3, 2002

We are at Kiddy Club Med in Ixtapa, Mexico. I decided to take Natasha on a vacation because it is close to our one-year anniversary. I met Natasha on February 21, 2001, and I asked her to be my daughter on February 22. And my birthday is on February 4. The trip served as an incentive for Natasha's good behavior. She had to get 20 smiley faces in order to go. I also wanted to make sure Natasha and I could have a vacation together before Nicolai arrives. Natasha's world is going to change a lot when he comes. I thought it would be good to have some good memories of our year together before he comes, and the family dynamics change.

I just went through the schedule of activities for kids and adults, and I've chosen to put Natasha in the mini club med from 9 a.m. to 4:30 p.m., then pick her up and go to the beach together. I will also let her participate in the show rehearsals. She loves the shows. I am surprised that most of the families here are couples. In fact, all the families with kids are couples.

February 9, 2002

Our vacation at Club Med is almost over. I thought that all the activity at Mini Club Med would physically tire out Natasha and that she would sleep perfectly through the night. I thought she would be happy and would be on good behavior. The opposite is true.

The Mini Club Med has plenty of activities, and she does finally tire out at 10:30 p.m. after the show, but she doesn't sleep calmly at night. In addition, Natasha's behavior has regressed about four to six months. The first night, Natasha woke up once and went back to sleep. Now, she has begun waking up two or three times a night, with loud crying. Her acting out also progressively worsened to that of a three-year-old, with lots of arguing. She has also been approaching lots of other mothers with open arms, like she did when we first came to United States. She is resisting me and not listening to anything I am saying. She is also demonstrating lots of nervous behavior, like putting her hair in her mouth, constantly chewing on her nails, eating with her fingers, and rocking back and forth with her hands in her crotch. Natasha is wound up like a tight top. Then on Wednesday night after the first show, she woke up screaming and crying twice and wet her bed (which hasn't happened for a very long time). It was like she was a volcano ready to explode. On Wednesday night, she exploded. The last couple of days I let her sleep in until 9 a.m. She has caught a cold, but her energy hasn't slowed down a bit.

Thinking that we were on vacation and there were so many fun activities to do, I didn't have a smiley face behavior program in place. I thought we wouldn't need one on this trip. On Wednesday night, I started to get concerned, and I asked other parents if their kids were more wound up than usual. They said a little, but mostly after four days of extra activity, they were getting tired sooner and going to bed earlier. While here, I befriended two women, a doctor and a spiritual healer and yoga instructor from Germany.

After I explained Wednesday night's incident to them, the doctor said it sounded like post-traumatic stress, and the yoga instructor said that it sounded like Natasha's soul was healing. It became very apparent to me that I need to get some professional advice on Natasha's sleep disorder and find out what is going on. All during our vacation, I've been trying desperately to figure out what is typical five-year-old behavior on a vacation, and what is happening in addition to that for Natasha. It's very difficult to figure it out. The interesting thing about this vacation is that I'm observing all the other families here with their kids. I am really questioning if I want any more children. I'm in awe of all the patience the other parents have. I'm also disappointed at the lack of discipline that I am seeing.

On the next trip, I will keep my smiley face program in place and substitute the shows or something she really wants to do as the reward. It would be interesting to see if it makes a difference. I also wonder if I should have come on vacation alone with my girlfriend and left Natasha with a babysitter. That would have been a true vacation. This is a 50 percent vacation for me.

I keep trying to figure out what is triggering Natasha's regression and stress. The only thing that I can think of is the lack of structure at the Mini Club Med. It's pretty free flowing with no time outs. I think the lack of structure, and the show preparation is triggering the past. At the orphanage, there was a big entertainment room where the kids would sing, dance and put on shows. Another idea could be the change of the environment and all the kids speaking a different language. One-third of the kids are speaking French, one-third English, one-third Spanish. When the kids are speaking a different language, Natasha asks me if they are speaking Russian. I am surprised because Natasha understands Russian, and she doesn't understand French or Spanish.

I am ready to go home. It was a good trip, but it is getting to be a little chaotic for me, and it scares me. It's two steps forward and one step back.

February 14, 2002

It's been four days since we returned from our trip to Ixtapa, Mexico. Things are finally settling down, and we are back to our routine. Natasha is starting to behave like normal again—like she did before we left for Mexico. The first couple of days back I wasn't sure if it was a great idea to have taken Natasha to Mexico. The regression was really bad and painful for me. I am meeting with my therapist on Friday to try to understand what was going on and if it's normal behavior for our situation. I do feel very hurt by Natasha, and I'm only slowly coming back. I did put up all sad faces on the calendar for the week we were in Mexico to remind Natasha of how not to treat Mama and smiley faces for her good behavior to continue to reinforce Natasha's good behavior. Natasha is still having sleeping problems. I have put a call into the director at the Children's Hospital International Adoption Clinic. His team did a comprehensive report on Natasha June 15, so I am calling him not only to find out how serious this is but also for an overall progress report.

February 15, 2002
(Therapist Session)

After I explained what happened on the trip, my therapist explained what had happened.

First of all, when I took Natasha out of the country, she didn't
know where she was. She was totally over-stimulated with
activities, people, language, food, shows, sports, scenery, etc.
She had no control or boundaries. She was bouncing off the
walls. I needed to regulate and control her because she was out
of control. She was aware, however, that she was a bad girl.
Natasha was experiencing anxiety at night, with languages,
families, not knowing where was she, and wondering if I was I
going to leave her there. All her behavior served to protect
herself and create safety for herself. The trance-like state she had
assumed was a result of over-stimulation and shock. She shut
down and could only let in small bits at a time to protect herself
from being over-stimulated. She said that Natasha's history and
background is not stable yet. There hasn't been enough time to
create stability.

This is not what I expected. Now that I think back on all the
trips we have taken, the same behavior has occurred—Boston,
Moldova, Bulgaria, and now Mexico. So now I must decide what
I will do on the next trip. The behavior probably won't change
very much. Do I want to deal with it or make arrangements to
leave Natasha at home? When we travel, I am emotionally
exhausted, and I'm doing the emotional work of two people.

The good news is that it is good for anxiety and confusion to
surface so that we can deal with it. Otherwise, it will be buried
and will surface later, causing larger problems. The term for
resisting authority or "not listening" is called "opposition."
Opposition means feeling out of control of your environment and
wanting to control everything in response to the internal chaos.
People in opposition also have a tendency to shut down when
over-stimulated. The only recourse is patience. Maintain the
boundaries and hang in there, even though it feels painful.
Natasha needs her familiar and consistent surroundings,
boundaries and structure.

After one week back, Natasha has said that she didn't like
Mexico because the bigger kids kept telling her that she was a
bad girl, probably because she was out of control, and they were
trying to keep her in line.

I learned some important lessons. Over-stimulation creates a wild child. A child in chaos is out of control. Children don't know how to control their emotions. A child doesn't have the skill set yet and needs an adult to control them and set boundaries. I need to do this even if she can only understand a raised voice, which for me creates anger and is emotionally exhausting.

February 27, 2002

The American Embassy approved Nicolai today for his fiancé visa. He made his airline reservations and is coming to Denver on April 2. He is wait-listed for April 1. The wedding invitations went out today, and all wedding plans were confirmed. The American wedding date is April 19.

Natasha is sleeping through the night now, and she is very happy to be home and in her routine. She is still having her moments, but it is apparent that she likes her home, her school, her friends and her routine. Natasha is going to her counseling sessions once a week, and the Children's Hospital has said that we are progressing nicely. We just need to give everything more time. They warned that there could be some major set backs when Nicolai comes because our regular routine will be disrupted for a while, and Natasha will have to share my attention, which she is not used to. But, in the long run, it is good for Natasha to have a father and she seems excited to have a larger family.

March 16, 2002

For the past month, most of my time has been spent getting ready for Nicolai's arrival and getting ready for the wedding. The wedding and reception will be at the Willshire Inn in Denver, Colorado. I'm expecting about 50 people to show up, mostly my family and friends. Nicolai's aunt will be coming to represent his family at the American wedding. I am also preparing in advance for the next round of INS documents for the week after we are married. We have to file an I485 package for temporary residency, Advanced Parole document (so Nicolai can go back to Russia to have a second wedding), and work permit.

I'm trying to get as much done as I can before Nicolai arrives. I feel my second adoption is arriving soon. The bedroom and bathroom is ready for his arrival. After he gets here, we will be running around getting a marriage license, talking to the justice of the peace, getting a Russian translation of marriage in the United States, visiting the English schools, setting up a checking account, getting a social security number, getting more INS pictures taken, etc. Then, maybe next year, we have the third adoption, Nicolai's daughter. All the same paperwork will have to be filed again.

It will be interesting to see how Natasha handles the wedding and all this change. She is excited, but all the experts warn me that there will probably be a lot of regression on her part. They insist that continued therapy during this transition is critical. Plus, I won't be surprised to see Nicolai in some of our therapy sessions. Thank God the therapist speaks Russian.

March 27, 2002

Six more days until Nicolai will be here. During the day, I'm excited and at night I wake up in the middle of the night at least once. I think my subconscious is stressing out. After I talk to Nicolai on the phone, then I sleep well for a couple of nights.

Last Friday Natasha and I had therapy sessions together with Lena, Natasha's therapist. We played together. Natasha wanted to be the teacher, and Lena and I were her students. Lena didn't know it, but I was acting exactly like Natasha, and Lena was Lena. This therapy ended up being a break-through session because after we left, Natasha cried hysterically. For about a month, Natasha has been saying that she doesn't want to play with Lena anymore. I found out that she doesn't want to play with Lena because it always makes her sad. I mentioned this to Lena, and she said that we are really getting somewhere, so it is best to continue.

Over the weekend, Natasha started asking who she is and where she is from and what happened to her parents. I was surprised and answered her as best as I could. I said that her mommy couldn't take care of her anymore, that there was no food, clothes, money or furniture, and that her grandmother had died. That is when Natasha was put in the Russian school to live, so she could get a new mommy and have food, school, and a better life. I said, "I am your new mama and soon you will have a new daddy and we will not leave you." Natasha summarized this whole message as, "My mama and daddy are gone. I lived in a castle in Russia, and my parents were killed, and now my life is here." I agreed, adding, "Later, when you are older, if you want, we can see if we can find someone." This didn't interest her now, but the part about my not leaving seems to help her feel safe.

On Monday, we had another therapy session with Lena. This time Natasha wanted to play games, and we were all friends. It was obvious that Natasha wanted me to be her best friend, and we left Lena out of the game a lot. Natasha had told Lena that she wants mama to play with Lena and her. Natasha said she isn't as scared with mama around. We let Natasha win and really built her up. Natasha felt great after this play session. When we went home, I asked Natasha if she felt sad. She said no.

Today, I debriefed with Lena on these sessions. She said that Natasha is really progressing and that we don't need to do much more therapy. We are going to keep at it for a while during the transition with Nicolai and see how that goes. Her suggestion is that we need to mourn the loss of her primary caretakers (grandmother and mother). So I will get a book on death for children, like *Cat Heaven*. I will then show her my grandmother's grave. And then we might be able to have a ceremony for her to grieve her loss. Lena says that this is something we will need to continue as she gets older and starts asking questions again. I am happy to have planted the first seed and feel ready to answer her questions.

March 31, 2002

It's Easter. Natasha is very excited that the Easter bunny came and ate his carrots that were laid out the night before on the kitchen table. She liked her Easter basket, Easter bunny and chocolate Easter egg hunt. In the morning Natasha was in good spirits, and I was surprised at her nice behavior. Natasha is excited to get dressed up to go to church. In fact, she put her fancy dress on at 8 a.m. even though church didn't start until 10:30 a.m. After sitting in her dress watching movies for two hours, we headed out to the Easter service. We were both disappointed to find out that there was no children's church, so we stuck it out for a 90-minute service. Afterward, we had brunch with friends and then went to my parents' house, where we had another chocolate Easter egg hunt and a turkey feast. I tried on my wedding dress for my parents and Natasha.

I can sense that Natasha is starting to regress and is starting to feel out of control because Nicolai will be arriving soon. She is starting to exhibit anxiety. I must admit that I am also. I think we are both excited and scared at the same time. This reminds me of how we were acting together when I was going to leave for Moscow last December to see Nicolai. Natasha keeps asking me, "Why does he have to come?" I think she is really starting to understand what is going on. At dinner with my parents, Natasha said a prayer, "Nicolai and Mama will be married soon, and I will wear a pink dress and throw flowers out of a basket with Kate and Shannon. Mama is my mama, and Nicolai will be my papa."

May 8, 2002

It's been five weeks since my fiancé arrived and we have been married for 18 days. My husband said he feels like he has been in the United States for six months. The wedding was a success. We ended up with 54 guests, including five from Russia. The wedding was a mix of American and Russian culture. The justice of the peace created a humorous ceremony using a book on Pushkin's poems, Natasha and her two girlfriends were great and beautiful flower girls, my uncle added "Gorko" (Russian tradition to kiss the bride) to the toast, and the reception ended with a traditional Russian dance show.

For the first three weeks that her new father was here, Natasha didn't want to have anything to do with him. She kept asking me privately, "When is he going to go back to Moscow?" My new husband decided to keep his distance until Natasha was ready to begin accepting him. After the wedding was over and all the houseguests were gone, Natasha slowly started warming up to her new father.

She is cautious but very curious about what her new father is doing and where he is. Natasha is now starting to play with Nicolai, and I think a friendship is slowly starting to form. Nicolai and I decided to wait until after the wedding and after a session with Lena (Natasha's therapist) before we made any changes, since the adjustment is going pretty smoothly—better than anticipated. Finally, I told Natasha that she and I are taking a break from therapy for a while. Lena said the work is done for now, but the door is always open for us to return.

So, this is the beginning of our new family. We have decided to postpone the Russian Orthodox Church wedding until the summer of 2003. My husband's daughter has decided to postpone living in the United States, and will begin studying at the University of Moscow in September of 2003.

Afterword

My first year with Natasha

Deciding to adopt Natasha is the largest decision I have ever made in my life. It has truly changed my life in ways I never could have imagined. I have completely re-structured my life to accommodate Natasha. I have never experienced so much emotional growth in such a short time. And I have had to learn to take each day as it comes and simply survive. When I thought, "I can't do this anymore," something would happen to give me the strength to continue. After one year, I am just starting to feel that I can breathe again. The beginning of a routine and structure is critical. And for me the support system has been essential. I have come to the realization that I am not cut out to be a 24-hour-a-day mom, but I can be a mom seven days a week with Monday through Friday's off from 9 a.m. to 5:30 p.m. And I need a weekend off once a month. I know I am a better mom and happier when I take time for myself without feeling guilty about it.

I now know where every playground is located near our house. I know all about Barbie, Powder Puff Girls, and Sailor Moon. I have taken a fresh look at Cinderella, Sleeping Beauty and Snow White, and I know that the local library is my new best friend for children's videos and books. I know a lot more about the Denver public school system. I am learning about how powerful imagination and drawing are to communicate with children. I now have great empathy for single mothers who are either widowed or who have no ex-husband support. I can't imagine having a full-time career without having a nanny. I am now a much better cook because I cook almost everyday. I am developing patience and more tolerance for child-like behavior. I like experiencing the miracle of Natasha learning: English, social skills, the alphabet and numbers, and, of course, her learning to attach.

I am asked if I had it to do all over again, would I adopt Natasha? I take a deep breath and say yes. It's a lot of work, and it sure isn't easy, but I don't want to live my life without experiencing this new world. Working with children and having your own are two different things. I think it's the ultimate responsibility that makes the difference. The pressure is on when this child's life and future is in your hands. I am responsible for the blueprint of her life, and I only get one chance. I don't just play with her or teach her, then give her back. I have to think of the short-term and long-term consequences of everything I do. And I want to do the best job I can.

The first year is the hardest one when adopting a foreign, older child. There are so many reasons: First, the language barrier and having to learn to communicate with each other immediately is very stressful, as is making up for lost time. Sometimes Natasha is three, and sometimes she is five. We have to make up for the time that she was in the orphanage and not in the "real world."

Second, the lifestyle change and time commitment is striking. It is extremely important that you realize that your lifestyle will change. It will take a minimum of six to 12 months to establish a routine that includes your friends or dating, if you are single.

Attachment and bonding are also major issues. It can be painful for you as a parent to hear your child say she doesn't want you. And I've discovered that the accelerated learning of how to be a mother is emotionally and physically exhausting. Simply being responsible for another person 24 hours a day is wearing.

For a single person, getting a support system is a high priority. It's important to get into a routine and structure that works for both parties. This takes time and can be quite difficult in the beginning. Finally, learning the balance between discipline and letting your child be a child.

If I had not met Natasha, I would never have met my husband. I feel Nicolai is the gift for adopting Natasha. All my life all I wanted was a family, and now one is forming. It certainly isn't forming in the traditional fashion, but it is forming in the way it is supposed to be.